LITERACY PLAY FOR THE EA

Book 3

Learning through poetry

COLLETTE DRIFTE

David Fulton Publishers

London

Dedicated to the memory of

Christopher Rowe (1942–2001)

whose poems and songs have brought pleasure to many children
and practitioners over the years

David Fulton Publishers Ltd
The Chiswick Centre, 414 Chiswick High Road, London W4 5TF

www.fultonpublishers.co.uk

David Fulton Publishers is a division of Granada Learning, part of the Granada Media Group.

First published in Great Britain by David Fulton Publishers 2003
10 9 8 7 6 5 4 3 2 1

British Library Cataloguing in Publication Data
A catalogue record for this book is available from the British Library.

ISBN: 1-85346-958-0

Also available in the **Literacy Play for the Early Years** series:

Book 1: *Learning through fiction* ISBN 1-85346-956-4
Book 2: *Learning through non-fiction* ISBN 1-85346-957-2
Book 4: *Learning through phonics* ISBN 1-85346-959-9

Cover design by Phil Barker
Designed and typeset by FiSH Books, London
Printed and bound in Great Britain by Thanet Press Limited, Margate, Kent

Contents

Acknowledgements iv

Introduction 1

1 *Pick 'N' Mix Zoo* by Celia Warren 6

2 *Humpty Dumpty* and *Little Miss Muffet* (Traditional) 15

3 *Three Purple Elephants* by Joan Poulson and *Early in the Morning* (Anonymous) 25

4 *Look at your hat!* and *In the cupboard* by Barbara Ireson 42

5 *When I Get Up in the Morning* by Clive Webster and *The Band* (Traditional) 53

6 *Sing a Song of Sixpence* and *Planting Beans* (Traditional) 67

7 *New Shoes* (Anonymous) and *I Don't Like Custard* by Michael Rosen 78

8 *Cousin Peter* (Traditional) and *Funny Jim* by Barbara Ireson and Christopher Rowe 94

Observation and assessment for speaking and listening 106

Observation and assessment for reading and writing 107

Acknowledgements

The author and publishers would like to thank the copyright holders of the following poems that were used in this book:

Pick 'N' Mix Zoo © Celia Warren 1996, first published in *First Verses* by John Foster (Oxford University Press 1996).

Three Purple Elephants © Joan Poulson 1996, first published in *Action Rhymes* by John Foster (Oxford University Press 1996).

Look at your hat! by Barbara Ireson, first published in *Over and Over Again* by Barbara Ireson and Christopher Rowe (Beaver Books 1978) and reprinted by kind permission of Patricia Rowe.

In the cupboard by Barbara Ireson, first published in *Over and Over Again* by Barbara Ireson and Christopher Rowe (Beaver Books 1978) and reprinted by kind permission of Patricia Rowe.

When I Get Up in the Morning © Clive Webster 1996, first published in *First Verses* by John Foster (Oxford University Press 1996).

I Don't Like Custard © Michael Rosen 1990, first published in *Never Mind* (BBC Books 1990) and reprinted by permission of PFD on behalf of Michael Rosen.

Funny Jim by Barbara Ireson and Christopher Rowe, first published in *Over and Over Again* by Barbara Ireson and Christopher Rowe (Beaver Books 1978) and reprinted by kind permission of Patricia Rowe.

I should like to thank the following for their support and encouragement throughout the writing of this book: Helen Fairlie of David Fulton Publishers for her sound suggestions and professional friendliness; Alan Worth, also of David Fulton Publishers, for seeing the book through the production process; Sophie Cox for her excellent copy-editing; friends and professionals who tried out the activities and made suggestions; the children's parents; and, finally, but probably most important of all, the children themselves. Some of them feature in the little scenarios but, for reasons of confidentiality, their names and details have been altered.

Collette Drifte

Introduction

Curriculum guidance for the foundation stage, the *National Literacy Strategy* and learning through play

Many early years practitioners find it difficult to reconcile the Early learning goals of the Foundation stage and the objectives of the *National Literacy Strategy* (DfEE 1998). The philosophy of learning through play is emphasised in *Curriculum guidance for the foundation stage* (DfEE 2000) and rightly so – it is beyond question that young children learn both more, and more effectively, through involvement in activities that are enjoyable, fun, and contain an element of play. The *National Literacy Strategy* (NLS) document outlines its objectives without touching on this in any depth and the practitioner may perhaps feel that it is a sterile document in terms of addressing the concept of learning through play. But the two documents aren't mutually exclusive and they can live alongside each other fairly well, since many of the NLS objectives do actually tie in with the Early learning goals.

For example:

Early learning goals from Curriculum guidance for the foundation stage, *Communication, language and literacy:*

- Listen with enjoyment, and respond to stories, songs and other music, rhymes and poems and make up their own stories, songs, rhymes and poems.
- Explore and experiment with sounds, words and texts.

Objectives from the National Literacy Strategy (YR) *:*

- To understand and be able to rhyme through recognising, exploring and working with rhyming patterns.
- To reread and recite stories and rhymes with predictable and repeated patterns and experiment with similar rhyming patterns.

Philip, Joel and Wesley enjoyed reciting *Humpty Dumpty Sat on a Chair* with the practitioner, doing some actions at the same time. (*Humpty Dumpty sat on a chair/ Eating ripe bananas./ Where do you think he put the skins?/ Down his new pyjamas!/* Anon.) They recited the rhyme several times together, with the practitioner pausing to let the children supply the last word of each line, or taking turns to recite a line each. Later the children decided to write an extension of the rhyme. They talked about the things that Humpty could sit on, including a motorbike and a horse, before settling on a swing. They also changed the fruit to oranges. They wrote their new poems on paper, using the original as a model and for support, and they illustrated it themselves before it was displayed on the wall. In this scenario, all the Foundation stage goals and NLS objectives listed above have been achieved.

Advisers and inspectors are recommending that early years practitioners give priority to the *Curriculum guidance for the foundation stage* in their setting, so the children should not lose out on either the stepping stones or the learning through play philosophy. As long as you plan your activities within the framework of *Curriculum guidance for the foundation stage*, you will still be addressing many of the NLS objectives when targeting the Early learning goals.

Some professionals working at the foundation stage, however, feel pressurised to teach towards the goals themselves, and are concerned that the stepping stones become overlooked. It is crucial that each child works at an appropriate level and is not pushed ahead too soon towards future outcomes. As professionals, therefore, we need to stand firm in our approach to working with all children at their own level, in their own time. By recording their achievements and showing why they are working on the current stepping stone, we will be able to illustrate the positive reasons for doing this.

Planned activities and appropriate intervention

A second debate to come out of the *Curriculum guidance for the foundation stage* is the principle it promotes of 'activities planned by adults' and 'appropriate intervention' to help the children in their learning (DfEE 2000: 11). Some practitioners feel that children should be left to learn through play, without any intervention by adults, while others may find themselves heavily directing the children's activities in order to highlight a learning point.

Most practitioners, though, would agree that the ideal is a balance between these two and the skill comes in knowing when and how to intervene, to maximise the children's learning opportunity. Leaving children to play freely in the belief that they will eventually learn the targeted skill or concept through discovery, assumes that learning is a sort of process of osmosis by which knowledge is automatically absorbed. This takes learning through play to a questionable extreme and will end up throwing the baby out with the bathwater – a child can play freely all day long without actually coming around to the learning point that the practitioner is aiming for. On the other hand, intervention can easily become interference – it can stifle children's exuberance and enthusiasm for the activity, because their curiosity and creativity are hampered by too much direction from the adult. This will never lead to effective learning. The practitioner needs to be sensitive as to when and how to intervene in the children's play, to help them discover the learning point.

In her book *Understanding Children's Play* (Nelson Thornes 2001), Jennie Lindon outlines the different roles that the professional plays when interacting with the child, including, for example, play companion, model, mediator, facilitator, observer-learner, etc. If you come to recognise which of these roles is appropriate to adopt in a given situation, you will go a long way to making sure children's learning is positive and successful, and fun. The skill lies in ensuring that structure and intervention are there in your planning, which in turn allows the children to determine the nature of the play.

Working towards literacy

When working to develop children's literacy skills, we need to bear in mind that literacy is not confined to reading and writing. All aspects of language as a whole, including speaking, listening, comprehension, expression and conversational skills, are crucial components of literacy. Without language, literacy skills can't be learnt. Speaking and listening feature largely in the *Curriculum guidance for the foundation stage* and so are acknowledged as the fundamental basis of the acquisition of literacy skills. While self-analysis and consideration of others' opinions are featured as objectives at a later stage of the *National Literacy Strategy*, children in the early years need to be introduced to these concepts. Paying attention to and taking account of others' views is part of the foundation stage work. Very young children have differing opinions as much as adults and older children, and they need to realise that opinions which are different from their own deserve to be respected and valued.

The reverse of this coin is that they should be able to develop the confidence to express their own opinion in the knowledge that it will be seen as a valuable contribution to the discussions held by the whole group. They must know that even if their opinion is different from others', it is a valid one and will be welcomed by everyone as an alternative view.

Imaginative play, creativity and role-play are also important elements in language development, and therefore in acquiring literacy skills. If we enable children to explore and play in imaginative situations, their ability to understand and enjoy fiction will be enhanced, as will their own creative literary abilities. Fiction and stories are, after all, only a different medium for expressing the creative play that goes on in every early years Home Corner!

Literacy (and language), as such, is not an isolated bubble or a 'subject' of the curriculum to be taught at specific times of the day. It cuts across every area of learning and is part of everything we do. While it is convenient for the sake of record keeping and planning to talk about 'Literacy', it's really something that can't be pigeon-holed or put onto a form with tick-boxes to record when we have 'done' it. It permeates every part of learning: reading the labels on maths equipment together may happen during a maths session, but it's still literacy; writing captions on the bottom of a painting links art and literacy.

So it soon becomes clear how using play, games and fun activities are ways we can approach literacy, enabling the children to develop the skills they need.

Who is this book for?

I hope that all early years practitioners will find something useful in this book and by 'all practitioners', I mean professionals who work in any capacity within the field of early years education. I have tried to use 'neutral' language in the book, i.e. not school-based terms, since the education of early years children takes place in many settings other than schools or nominated educational establishments. Although I have explored some of the issues involved in the *Curriculum guidance for the foundation stage/National Literacy Strategy* debate, this is not to say the implications are only for schools. I would argue that they affect everyone providing education for young children and so the issues are just as relevant to non-school settings. But aside from this, I hope that the book will be useful to practitioners thanks to the practical nature of the ideas and suggestions. The activities can be done either within the framework of a session aiming for one of the official curriculum targets, or as a non-curriculum session with the setting's own aims in view. Of course, the activities are only suggestions, and practitioners could easily adapt or change them to suit their own situation.

What's in the book?

This book explores a variety of poems and how they can be used as the basis of activities that are fun and contain an element of play, yet still have a literacy skill as the target. While speaking and listening remain integral elements to every session, I have chosen to focus on either reading or writing poetry in any one session. Young children often find difficulty in sitting still for long periods of time in a more formal situation, and focusing on both reading and writing poetry in one go would demand this.

There is both modern and traditional poetry included in the book. I make no apology for using some of the old favourites since there are always new practitioners and new children entering early years settings, who will enjoy exploring these in more depth for the first time. The veterans of the game will know that the children who are familiar with the poems never tire of hearing them over and over again, often reciting them perfectly themselves!

There are two observation and assessment sections at the end of the book to give the practitioner an idea of what to look for when the children are working to acquire a specific skill. These sections are by no means exhaustive and practitioners can 'pick and mix' the elements that are most useful to them, adding anything that they may feel needs to be included. I can't stress enough the importance of observation as a tool for assessment, since so much can be gathered of a child's achievements, progress and performance by this simple but extremely effective practice. The stepping stones in the *Curriculum guidance for the foundation stage* can also provide a useful guide to the child's achievements, particularly as the colour bands help to put the stepping stones into an age-related context. But we need to remember that they are just that – a guide to the child's progress en route to the Early learning goals – and not be tempted to use them as an assessment or teaching tool as such.

There are also some photocopiable pages which are linked in with the activities. These are not worksheets to be given to the children to 'do', but are a resource to save the practitioner preparation time. They must be used by the adult and the children working together on the activity, in a fun way without pressure.

What's in a chapter?

Each chapter follows the same format, with suggestions for two sessions, one focusing on reading poetry and the other focusing on writing it. The basic framework of each chapter is as follows:

- One or two featured poems – the title(s) and the poet(s).
- Early learning goals from *Curriculum guidance for the foundation stage*, which are relevant to the chapter's focus.
- Objectives from the *National Literacy Strategy*, which link in with the Early learning goals.
- Materials needed – everything needed to do the session and activities.
- Optional materials for other activities – a list of resources needed for the other structured play activities.
- Preparation – details of what needs to be done beforehand. This often includes something like *Make a set of picture matching cards using Photocopiable Sheet 5*. The most effective way of doing this is to photocopy the sheet, stick it onto card and when the glue is dry, cut the sheet into the individual cards. You might like to ask the children to colour those cards that have pictures. You could laminate the cards for future use and to protect against everyday wear and tear.
- Introducing the poem – for you as the practitioner either with everyone together or in groups, as you require. Although this section has been scripted, this is for guidance only and naturally you should present the material in your own 'style'. There may be questions asked and issues explored in this section which you feel aren't appropriate for your children's achievement level. The flexibility of the session means that you can 'pick and mix' those bits that *are* relevant to your own situation, leaving out what you don't want, or exploring further something that may be looked at in less detail than you'd like. There may be times when you prefer to explore a poem together over several sessions and therefore you might only use part of this section each time.
- Focus activities – these can be done in whichever way you prefer, e.g. adult-led, in groups, independent, child-selected, etc. They have been designed to cater for different achievement levels and obviously you should 'pick and mix' as you require. You could adapt, add to or ignore them according to your own setting's needs. Some of the games have a competitive element in them, for example by winning tokens or avoiding 'elimination'. These can be adapted, if you prefer, to leave out that element of the game, in which case the children's satisfaction at their own achievement is the outcome of the activity.

- Other structured play activities – suggestions for other things to do as an 'optional extra'. They bring in wider aspects of Early learning goals and the NLS objectives, beyond the chapter's main focus. Some of the activities are competitive but, as mentioned above, you can adapt them to leave out this element if you prefer.
- The poem(s) featured in the chapter.
- Related photocopiable sheets.

CHAPTER 1

Pick 'N' Mix Zoo

by Celia Warren (p. 13)

Early learning goals from *Curriculum guidance for the foundation stage*, Communication, language and literacy:

- Listen with enjoyment, and respond to . . . rhymes and poems . . .
- Use language to imagine and recreate roles and experiences.
- Explore and experiment with sounds, words and texts.

Objectives from the *National Literacy Strategy (YR)*:

- To understand and be able to rhyme through recognising, exploring and working with rhyming patterns.
- To have a knowledge of grapheme/phoneme correspondence through hearing and identifying initial sounds in words.
- To use a capital letter for the start of own name.

Materials needed

- Enlarged version of the poem (see 'Preparation') and the copy on p. 13
- Easel and Blu-tack
- A bag of pick 'n' mix sweets, if possible including some of the varieties in the poem
- The children's name cards
- Flip-chart and marker pens
- A set of cards with the words from the poem on them (see 'Preparation')
- Photocopiable Sheet 1 (p. 14) made into a set of cards (see 'Preparation')
- Plastic alphabet letters – *b, c, e, h, k, l, m, p* and *s*. You could add a few more that aren't needed if the children can manage an extra challenge
- Tokens
- Paper, paint, brushes, etc. for pictures of some of the animals
- Paper and pencils for labels or captions

Optional materials for other activities

- Ingredients listed in the recipe(s) in Figures 1.1 and 1.2 (pp. 11 and 12), cooking utensils, children's aprons/overalls
- Card, scissors, string, paint and brushes to make masks
- A selection of books related to zoos or wild animals
- Picture cards made from Photocopiable Sheet 1 (p. 14)
- Feely bag
- Shoe boxes or similar, malleable materials (e.g. plasticine, play dough, etc.) and model junk (e.g. empty packets, boxes, cardboard tubes, old wrappings, egg boxes, etc.) to make the pick 'n' mix stall. (Check whether any of the children have allergies, to avoid triggering a problem from minute traces of food that may be in the junk.)

Preparation

▲ Put the sweets into the feely bag.

▲ Either enlarge the poem (p. 13) on a photocopier or type it on a computer using 26-point Tahoma with 1.5 line spacing, then print it out. Fix it to the easel and cover it up.

▲ Write on the flip-chart 'drops' and 'lollipops', 'bears' and 'hares', 'kangaroo' and 'zoo' and cover it up.

▲ Type the poem on a computer using 48-point Tahoma with double spacing and then print it out. The poem will be distorted, but don't worry because you only want the individual words. Stick the sheets onto card and then cut out each word (except for 'Red jelly', which should be kept together).

▲ Make a set of cards using Photocopiable Sheet 1 (p. 14), either for the group as a whole, or for each child in the group, as you require.

▲ Collect the ingredients for making peppermint creams and toffee (see Figures 1.1 and 1.2).

Introducing the poem

• Hold up the feely bag and ask the children to guess what might be in it – spiders, screws, pencils? Have some fun with the suggestions they make. When they guess 'sweets', spend a bit of time talking about the sweets in the bag. Which are their favourites? Why? Which sweets don't they like? Why not? Are any of the sweets new to the children? Explore them by talking about the colour, size, shape, taste and so on.

• Do they know what 'pick 'n' mix' means? Have they ever bought sweets from a pick 'n' mix stall? Do they know of other things we can pick 'n' mix as well as sweets? (For example, a salad bar in the supermarket or the mini-toys in toy hypermarkets.)

• Tell the children you're going to share a poem about pick 'n' mix. Read from the small version, letting the children enjoy the idea of sweetie-animals. When you've finished, ask them whether they liked the poem. Were they surprised to find it's about a zoo? Why or why not? Do they know what a zoo is? Let some of them talk about their visits to the zoo. Which is their favourite animal? Why? Are there any animals that the children don't like? Why not?

• Who can remember some of the sweetie-animals in the poem? Tell the children you're going to read the poem again and they should listen for any sweetie-animals they forgot to tell you about. Which animal in the poem is their favourite? Why? Can they make up some more sweetie-animals? For example, candy-floss kittens, popcorn penguins or chocolate chimpanzees.

• Can anyone tell you some words in the poem that sound the same ('drops' and 'lollipops', 'bears' and 'hares', 'kangaroo' and 'zoo')? Do the children know the word we use when words sound the same like this ('Rhyme')? Can they tell you some words that rhyme with those in the poem? For example, with 'drops' and 'lollipops' they could have 'shops', 'mops', 'stops' and 'hops'; with 'kangaroo' and 'zoo' they could have 'shoe', 'glue', 'stew' and 'two'.

• Help the children to make up some actions to represent each of the animals in the poem and practise them for a few moments. Then uncover the enlarged version of the poem and read it again to the children. Point to each word in the text as you say it, making sure your finger doesn't lag behind or run ahead as you read.

• Ask the children to help you design a logo or picture to show the action for each animal and draw it beside each line. Before you recite the poem together, make sure the children understand the logos. Leave the enlarged version pinned up for the children to explore in their own time.

Focus activities

Group A: Spread out one set of the poem's enlarged words on the table face up. Let the children look at the enlarged copy of *Pick 'N' Mix* and ask them to put the words together again to make each line of the poem. If the children can manage, you could let them play a form of pelmanism by pairing the words to make a line – you may have to limit this to words from fewer verses.

Group B: Give the children their name cards and ask them what sound their name begins with. Can they think of an animal and/or sweets starting with their own initial letter, in the style of the poem? For example, Thomas = toffee turtles; Catherine = crocodile crisps. If they find it difficult to find sweets to match their names, let them choose sweets that aren't alliterative, e.g. Pritpal = jelly-baby penguins. Let them write and draw their sweetie-animals (or scribe for them).

Group C: Let the group work at the uncovered flip-chart. Read the rhyming words together again and then have fun thinking of more words for each rhyming family. For example, to the 'bears' and 'hares' family they could add 'pears' ('pairs'!), 'stairs', 'cares', 'wears', etc. What's their world record number of rhymes? Leave the page open and let the children add to it as they think of more rhymes later.

Group D: Let the children make portraits of some of the animals in the poem. Encourage them to use bright colours – pink or yellow for the marshmallow monkeys, scarlet for the red jelly elephants, pink or green for the peppermint pandas, any colours they like for the candy kangaroo, and bright red and green for the strawberry snakes. Help them to write a label or caption for their pictures, and then make a display.

Group E: Give the picture cards from Photocopiable Sheet 1, tokens and the plastic alphabet letters to the group. They should take turns to put the correct initial letter on a card and if they are right, they win a token. The winner is the child with the highest number of tokens at the end of the game.

Other structured play activities

- Make some peppermint creams or toffee (see recipes on pp. 11 and 12) with the children. Leave one or two of the sweets beside a picture of a panda or a hippopotamus, along with a copy of the poem. (You might have to put up a sign that says 'Do not eat'!) Help the children to write labels saying 'peppermint creams' or 'toffee'. Check whether any of the children are allergic to any of the ingredients and be vigilant of the children when hot things are around. Remind them to put on their aprons and wash their hands first.
- Make animal masks with the children, for each of the animals in Celia Warren's poem. Let the children role-play the poem while wearing the masks.
- Put the picture cards made from Photocopiable Sheet 1 into the feely bag. Play a game where the children take a card out of the bag and look at the picture, without letting those around them see. They then mime actions of the animal and the others have to guess which one it is.
- Take the children into the hall or large play area and have some fun playing at being each of the animals in the poem. Encourage the children to think how each animal moves, sounds, looks and so on.
- Make a pick 'n' mix stall in the Home Corner using the shoe boxes. Let the children explore the sweets mentioned in Celia Warren's poem and make some for the stall using malleable materials. Let them role-play in the stall when they have finished.

Pick 'N' Mix Zoo

by Celia Warren (p. 13)

Early learning goals from *Curriculum guidance for the foundation stage*, Communication, language and literacy:

- Listen with enjoyment to, and respond to...rhymes and poems and make up their own...rhymes and poems.
- Use language to imagine and recreate roles and experiences.
- Explore and experiment with sounds, words and texts.

Objectives from the *National Literacy Strategy (YR)*:

- To use experience of...poems...as a basis for independent writing...
- To identify alliteration in known and new...words.
- To have a knowledge of grapheme/phoneme correspondence through hearing and identifying initial sounds in words.

Materials needed

- Enlarged version of the poem (see 'Preparation')
- Sticky notes
- Easel and Blu-tack
- Marker pens
- Flip-chart
- The children's name cards
- Stopwatch or clock with a second hand
- A set of cards with the words from the poem on them (see 'Preparation')
- Animal picture cards (see 'Preparation')
- Tokens
- Paper, pencils, coloured pens

Optional materials for other activities

- Big Book of nursery rhymes
- Plastic alphabet letters and a feely bag
- Cards with one line of a nursery rhyme on each – to make these, type out the rhyme on a computer using 26-point Tahoma with 1.5 line spacing, then print it out, stick it onto card and cut out each line
- Paper, paints, brushes, coloured pens, etc. for making pictures

Preparation

- ▲ Either enlarge the poem (p. 13) on a photocopier or type it on a computer using 26-point Tahoma with 1.5 line spacing, then print it out. Pin it to the easel.
- ▲ Type the poem into a computer using 48-point Tahoma with double spacing, then

print it out. The poem will be distorted, but don't worry because you only want the individual words. Stick the sheets onto card and then cut out each word (except for 'Red jelly', which should be kept together).

▲ Make cards using Photocopiable Sheet 1 (p. 14).

Introducing the poem

- Remind the children of *Pick 'N' Mix Zoo*. Enjoy reciting it together, with the children doing the actions they made up in the earlier session.
- What do they notice about Marshmallow monkeys, Lion lollipops, Caramel camels, Butterscotch bears, Peppermint pandas, Candy kangaroo and Strawberry snakes (i.e. the alliteration)?
- Blank off 'monkeys', 'crocodile' and 'lion' with the sticky notes. Can the children suggest alliterative alternatives? For example, 'mice', 'cat', 'ladybird'. Write their ideas on the flip-chart and then choose the substitutes. Write these on each sticky note then recite the new verse together.
- Tell the children you're all going to add some lines to the poem. Together, choose some animals and then decide on an alliterative word for each one – the words don't have to be sweets, but can be any food, providing the initial letter is the same, for example tomato tigers, cherry chimpanzees and so on.
- Write their ideas on the flip-chart before agreeing which ones to use for the additional verse. Let the children dictate the order of the verse, while you scribe.
- Recite the whole poem together once more (with actions), including the substitutes and adding the newly written verses.

Focus activities

Group A: Give the group the set of the poem's enlarged words. Let the children mix up the words to make variations in the *Pick 'N' Mix* style. For example, 'Marshmallow elephants', 'Red jelly hares' or 'Butterscotch monkeys'. Help the children to write their new animals as a line, a verse or a poem, either individually or in a group, as you wish.

Group B: Put the tokens and the animal picture cards face down on the table. Play a game where the children turn over a card and say an alliterative word to go with the picture. It doesn't have to make sense, as long as the initial sound is the same. If they're right they win a token, the winner being the child with the most tokens at the end of the game.

Group C: Give the children their name cards. Let them all think of a describing word beginning with each child's initial (let any of them 'pass' if they find it difficult). For example, 'clever Cathy', 'marvellous Manjit', 'brilliant Benjamin' and so on. You could add a challenge by using the stopwatch and a given time, for example one minute per name to get as many words as possible.

Group D: Use the sticky notes to blank off the animals in verse two of *Pick 'N' Mix Zoo*. Help the children to choose substitutes and make another new verse. Let the children write the new verse themselves or scribe for them. Add it to the verse written before and practise reciting the two new verses together.

Group E: With the children, make up some alliterative phrases using animals and numbers one to five. For example, 'One wombat', 'two terrapins', 'three thrushes', 'four foxes' and 'five frogs'. (Be careful to use the 'w' sound for 'one' rather than the letter 'o'.) Try adding an adjective to each example such as 'woolly', 'terrible', 'thumping', 'frisky' and 'funny'. Let the children draw their animals (the right number!) and write labels or captions for each one. You might need to scribe for them.

Other structured play activities

- Using the Big Book of nursery rhymes, have fun thinking of some new alliterative first lines together. For example, 'Hopeless Humpty sat in the hall' or 'Baa baa black sheep, bump and bounce the ball'.
- Put the plastic alphabet letters in a feely bag and let the children lucky-dip a letter. Help them to make up an alliterative phrase or sentence with it. For example, if they take out 's', they could say, 'Six silly sailors sitting in the sea'.
- Let the children play with the nursery rhyme 'one line' cards to make new rhyme openings by mixing up the lines. For example, 'Baa baa black sheep sat on a tuffet', 'Little Boy Blue have you any wool?' and so on.
- Encourage the children to illustrate their new versions of *Pick 'N' Mix Zoo*. Let them write the lines that go with their pictures, or scribe for them. Make a display of their work.

Peppermint creams

Ingredients

450g sieved icing sugar
1 tablespoon sweetened condensed milk
A few drops of peppermint oil (not essence)

Method

Mix the sugar and condensed milk together to a pliable dough. Knead well. Add a few drops of peppermint oil and knead to mix. Roll out onto a board sprinkled with icing sugar and cut into small rounds. Alternatively, roll small balls in the hand and then flatten them on the sugared board. Put to one side until firm.

Figure 1.1 How to make peppermint creams

Toffee

Ingredients

50g butter   ½ teaspoon lemon essence
220g demerara sugar   icing sugar
220g golden syrup

Method

Grease an oblong baking tin. Melt the butter and stir in the sugar and syrup. Bring to the boil and boil fast for ten minutes, stirring all the time. Remove from the heat and add the lemon essence. Pour into the greased tin and before it turns hard, mark it in squares with a knife. Leave to cool and break it into pieces when set hard.

NOTE: ENSURE THAT ALL CHILDREN ARE CAREFUL WHEN NEAR TO THE BOILING MIXTURE AND MAKE SURE THAT LITTLE FINGERS ARE KEPT WELL AWAY FROM THE MOLTEN TOFFEE!

Figure 1.2 How to make toffee

Pick 'N' Mix Zoo

Celia Warren

Marshmallow monkeys,
Crocodile drops,
Red jelly elephants,
Lion lollipops.

Caramel camels,
Butterscotch bears,
Toffee hippopotamus,
Chocolate hares.

Peppermint pandas,
Candy kangaroo,
Strawberry snakes
at the Pick 'n' Mix Zoo.

monkey   crocodile   elephant

lion   bear   hippopotamus

panda   kangaroo   snake

CHAPTER 2

FOCUS
Reading
poetry

Humpty Dumpty (p. 21), plus other traditional rhymes you might like to explore

Early learning goals from *Curriculum guidance for the foundation stage*, Communication, language and literacy:

- Listen with enjoyment, and respond to...rhymes and poems...and make up their own...rhymes and poems.
- Know that print carries meaning and, in English, is read from left to right and top to bottom.
- Show an understanding of the elements of stories, such as main character, sequence of events, and openings...

Objectives from the *National Literacy Strategy (YR)*:

- To track the text in the right order, page by page, left to right, top to bottom, pointing while you read/tell a story, and making one-to-one correspondence between written and spoken words.
- To identify rhyming words in nursery rhymes.
- To use knowledge of familiar texts to re-enact or retell to others, recounting the main points in the correct sequence.

Materials needed

- ■ Big Book of nursery rhymes including *Humpty Dumpty* (edition of your choice)
- ■ Flip-chart and marker pens
- ■ Acetate sheets
- ■ Marker pens in different colours
- ■ Set of rhyming picture cards (see 'Preparation')
- ■ Tokens
- ■ Large sheets of paper
- ■ Coloured pens
- ■ Set of 'starter word' cards for rhyming families (see 'Preparation')
- ■ Magnetic boards and letters
- ■ Cassette of pre-recorded everyday sounds
- ■ Cassette player
- ■ Enlarged versions of a selection of nursery rhymes

Optional materials for other activities

- A selection of books with traditional rhymes
- Large sheets of paper, coloured team bands
- Paints, brushes or felt pens (according to choice)
- Coloured pens
- Rhyming picture and/or word cards
- Cassette of recorded nursery rhymes
- Cassette player

Preparation

▲ Make a set of rhyming picture cards using Photocopiable Sheet 2 (p. 22).
▲ Make a set of 'starter word' cards using Photocopiable Sheet 3 (p. 23).
  (You could laminate the cards for future use and to protect against wear and tear.)
▲ Select and enlarge on a photocopier the nursery rhymes you want to use.

Introducing the poem

- Show the Big Book of nursery rhymes to the children and tell them you're going to explore some of the rhymes together. Let the children choose one of the nursery rhymes (not *Humpty Dumpty*) and share it, encouraging the children to join in. As you read, track the words with your finger, making sure you don't lag behind or run ahead of the words.

- Can anyone tell you which way we follow words when we read? If they don't know 'left' and 'right', let them show you by demonstrating. Who knows where we start to read a page? Who can tell you where it finishes? Explain that in English, all writing is like this.

- Look at *Humpty Dumpty* and discuss the illustration first. Do they like the picture? Why or why not? Make sure that the children respect 'negative' opinions and accept them as much as 'positive' ones – explain to them that it's fine to say they don't like something.

- Share the rhyme, tracking the words and encouraging the children to join in with you as you read. Make sure you point to each word as you say it, i.e. don't let your finger lag behind or go ahead.

- Can anyone tell you which words in *Humpty Dumpty* rhyme ('wall'/'fall' and 'men'/'again')? Encourage the children to come and point to the words as well as say them.

- Put the acetate sheet over the rhyme and draw a circle around each set of rhyming words, using a different colour for each set, (e.g. 'wall'/'fall' in red and 'men'/'again' in blue). See if they can tell you other words that are in the same rhyming family (e.g. 'call'/'small'/'tall'/'hall' and 'pen'/'ten'/'hen'/'when', etc.). Write their words on the flip-chart alongside those from the nursery rhyme.

- Ask the children how the story of *Humpty Dumpty* starts. What happens next? How does it finish? Do the children retell the story in the right sequence? Choose some of the children to act the roles of Humpty and a few King's horses and men, while you all say the rhyme together again.

- As a group, choose a different rhyme in the Big Book. Can the children identify the rhyming words in this one? Let them come out and circle the words with the coloured pens. How many other words can they think of which are in the same rhyming families? Write their words on the flip-chart and leave them up.

Focus activities

Group A: Let the children choose a rhyme from the Big Book. Help them to find the rhyming words and then get them to tell you other words in the same rhyming family. Together, make 'rhyming family charts' on the large sheets of paper, using different colours for each 'family'. Encourage the children to write the words (or scribe for them) and illustrate them. Display their charts on the wall.

Group B: Give the children the rhyming picture cards and ask them to sort the cards into rhyming pairs. Any child who can tell you another word that rhymes with each pair wins a token. The winner is the child with the highest number of tokens at the end of the game.

Group C: Sit with the children in a circle and start a round of words that rhyme, asking everyone to add a word – nonsense words are allowed. Some good starter words are 'peg', 'can', 'win' and 'sat'. You might like to start a slow regular clapping first to get the children into the rhythm – on each clap, say a rhyming word and then pass the turn to the next child. Each child adds his or her word on the following clap. (If any of the children find this hard, tell them to 'pass' until they're ready to join in.)

Group D: Listen to the tape of everyday sounds and take turns to identify a sound. Next ask the children for words (including nonsense ones) that rhyme with the name of whatever they can hear, including nonsense words, e.g. for 'cat', the children might say 'hat', 'mat', 'yat', 'zat' and so on. Give the children a token for each correct rhyme – the winner is the person with the most tokens at the end of the game.

Group E: Give the 'starter word' cards to the children and ask them to make rhyming families with the magnetic boards and letters. For example, for the 'starter word' 'pat', they might make 'bat', 'hat', 'cat' or 'fat'. Tell them they could even make nonsense words as long as they rhyme, e.g. 'gat', 'lat' and so on.

Other structured play activities

- Write one rhyming family word (e.g. 'hat', 'pen', 'sit', 'leg', etc.) on four sheets of paper and pin one on each wall in the hall. Divide the coloured team bands between the children. Play a game where you call out a colour and a word in one of the rhyming families. The children wearing that colour run to the wall with the rhyming word. For example, if you were to call out 'Yellow – cat', the children wearing yellow bands would run to the wall with 'hat' pinned up on it. You may prefer to use the actual word, i.e. 'hat', rather than others in the rhyming family.

- Using a stopwatch or egg timer, play a game with the children where you make the 'biggest' rhyming families possible before the sand runs out. Use the 'starter word' cards from Photocopiable Sheet 3 for this. Can the children beat their own record?

- Share the enlarged versions of the nursery rhymes, having fun reading them and encouraging the children to join in. Then pin the acetate sheets over them and help the children to circle the rhyming words in one colour for each rhyming family. Make up some more words, including nonsense words, for each rhyming family.

- Give the children the nursery rhyme cassette, the cassette player and an accompanying book. Let them play the tape, sing the rhymes and look at the book.

Little Miss Muffet
(Traditional) (p. 21)

Early learning goals from *Curriculum guidance for the foundation stage*, Communication, language and literacy:

• Listen with enjoyment, and respond to...rhymes and poems and make up their own ... rhymes and poems.
• Explore and experiment with sounds, words and texts.
• Attempt writing for different purposes using features of different forms...

Objectives from the *National Literacy Strategy (YR)*:

• Through shared writing to apply knowledge of letter/sound correspondence in helping the teacher to scribe, and rereading what the class has written.
• To think about and discuss what they intend to write, ahead of writing it.
• To use experience of stories, poems and simple recounts as a basis for independent writing.

Materials needed

■ Big Book of nursery rhymes including *Little Miss Muffet* (edition of your choice)
■ Two large copies of the rhyme (see 'Preparation')
■ Easel or board to display these
■ Flip-chart (or whiteboard) and marker pens
■ Paper, pencils and pens
■ Copy of Photocopiable Sheet 4 on p. 24 (see 'Preparation')
■ Card, scissors and glue
■ Copies of *Little Jack Horner*, *Little Miss Muffet* and *Jack and Jill* (see 'Preparation')
■ Blu-tack

Optional materials for other activities

■ Selection of nursery rhyme books
■ Paper, paint, brushes, coloured markers, etc. for picture making
■ Cassette recorder and blank cassette

Preparation

▲ Enlarge *Little Miss Muffet* by typing it on a computer using 28-point Tahoma with double spacing and then print it out. Delete the words 'tuffet', 'curds', 'whey' and 'spider', but leave spaces for substitutes. Make two copies. Fix one to the easel and cover it up. (The other one is for a group activity.)
▲ Make word/picture cards using Photocopiable Sheet 4 (p. 24). Put each set into a separate envelope, matched by the symbol in the corner of each card.
▲ Type *Little Jack Horner*, *Little Miss Muffet* and *Jack and Jill* on the computer using 22-point Tahoma with double spacing, and then print them out. Stick them onto card and cut out each line of the rhymes to make a set of eight one-line cards.

Introducing the poem

- Open the Big Book at *Little Miss Muffet* and share it with the children, encouraging them to join in. Spend a few minutes talking about the rhyme. Do they know what a tuffet is? What are curds and whey? Why was Miss Muffet frightened away? Would they have run away? Why or why not? If not a spider then what would make them run away?
- Tell the children that now you're all going to write some more of the poem, and it's going to be about what else might have happened to Miss Muffet. Remind the children that their new poem doesn't have to rhyme.
- Uncover the first enlarged version and read it through with the children, showing them where the gaps need new words. Help them to focus on the first space, where 'tuffet' should be.
- Ask the children what else Miss Muffet might have sat on, sensible or silly things, e.g. a sofa, a donkey or a tractor. Make a list of their ideas on the flip-chart and then choose one together. Write it in the right space on the enlarged copy.
- Next, ask the children what Miss Muffet might be eating instead of curds and whey, e.g. fish and chips, beans on toast, ham and eggs. Again, list their suggestions and choose one for the next spaces on the poem.
- Finally, think of some things that might have sat down beside Miss Muffet (not necessarily things that scare us), e.g. a hedgehog, a giant, a robot. Let the children choose one from the list and add it to the text. When you have finished the verse, read it together, encouraging the children to join in. This is an example of a new version:

> Little Miss Muffet sat on a bicycle
> Eating some egg and chips;
> There came a great monkey
> That sat down beside her
> And frightened Miss Muffet away.

- Tell the children that, if they wanted to, they could write as many verses as they wish. If they wrote a verse for each child it could be a very long nursery rhyme indeed!
- Recite the original rhyme together again and carry on with the new verse you all wrote together.
- Leave the new verse up for the group activities.

Focus activities

Group A: Give the children the second enlarged copy of *Little Miss Muffet*, with the missing words. Work together to write another new verse for the rhyme. Help them to brainstorm ideas and then choose one together. Let them know that they can change their minds if they're not happy at the end. (While drafting and redrafting are objectives at a later stage of the NLS, young children can be introduced to the concept.) If they need a bit of help, they could look at the poem written in the first session.

Group B: Use the word/picture cards (from Photocopiable Sheet 4) to play a game with the children. Let them have a 'lucky dip' from each envelope, which will give them substitute words for the rhyme. Then have fun saying the rhyme together with the new words. For example, they might pull out 'horse', 'sausage and chips' and 'caterpillar', so giving the rhyme:

Little Miss Muffet sat on a horse
Eating her sausage and chips;
There came a great caterpillar
That sat down beside her
And frightened Miss Muffet away.

Group C: Have some fun together making up actions to go with the rhyme. If the children prefer to use another rhyme, let them choose one from the Big Book. Help them to practise putting their new actions to the rhyme. Encourage them to give a performance for the others, and then teach them the actions as well.

Group D: Together choose another rhyme and write a second verse. Here are some ideas:

Sing a Song of Sixpence – a pocketful of what? What's baked in the pie?
   What happened when the pie was opened?
1, 2, 3, 4, 5 – what did I catch alive? What did I do with it? Why?
Little Jack Horner – what was he eating? What did he pull out? What did he say?
This Old Man – going up to five, what did he play at each number?

Group E: With the one-line cards made from *Little Jack Horner, Little Miss Muffet* and *Jack and Jill*, play around to make new rhymes. Show the children how this time they're changing whole lines, not just words. For example,

Jack and Jill went up the hill
Eating her curds and whey;
He put in his thumb and pulled out a plum
And Jill came tumbling after.

Use Blu-tack to stick the final version of the poem onto the easel. Depending on achievement level, the children could write out their new poem.

Other structured play activities

- If your local supermarket sells curds and/or whey, go on a shopping trip with the children and buy some. (Delicatessens or health food shops may also supply them.) Give the children an interesting experience by letting them have a taste of some 'unusual' foods. Remind them to wash their hands first. (Check beforehand whether any of the children have an allergy to dairy products.)
- Let the children paint or draw pictures to illustrate the new verse of *Little Miss Muffet* that you all wrote together. Make a display of their work on the wall and pin the rhyme up with the pictures.
- Play charades with the children, letting them choose a nursery rhyme character and mime actions to show who they are. The others should try to guess, with the successful 'guesser' taking the next turn.
- Put a selection of nursery rhyme books in the Book Corner for the children to explore. Give them time to do this without pressure – they'll gain as much by browsing through and discussing books together as in an adult-led activity. Encourage them to make up new verses for some of the rhymes. They could record their new versions onto a cassette.
- Turn the Home Corner into 'Nursery Rhyme Land' by putting in big beanbags, large building blocks, dressing-up clothes, soft toys and so on. Encourage the children to role-play the characters in their favourite nursery rhymes.

Humpty Dumpty

Traditional

Humpty Dumpty sat on a wall

Humpty Dumpty had a great fall

All the King's horses and all the King's men

Couldn't put Humpty together again.

Little Miss Muffet

Traditional

Little Miss Muffet sat on a tuffet

Eating her curds and whey,

Along came a spider that sat down beside her

And frightened Miss Muffet away.

hat	leg
man	tin
pen	pot

seesaw ●   bicycle ●   horse ●

sausage and chips ■   birthday cake ■   apples and pears ■

caterpillar ▲   hedgehog ▲   lion ▲

Three Purple Elephants

by Joan Poulson (p. 36)

Early learning goals from *Curriculum guidance for the foundation stage*, Communication, language and literacy:

- Interact with others, negotiating plans and activities and taking turns in conversation.
- Sustain attentive listening, responding to what they have heard by relevant comments, questions or actions.

Objectives from the *National Literacy Strategy (YR)*:

- To understand that words can be written down to be read again for a wide range of purposes.
- To read on sight a range of familiar words.

Materials needed

- Enlarged version of *Three Purple Elephants* (see 'Preparation'), easel, Blu-tack
- Flip-chart, coloured marker pens
- Cardboard rolls, string, paint, paintbrushes, plastic headbands, card, scissors, glue
- Red, blue, white and black paint, paintbrushes, paper, mixing pots or trays
- Animal cards, colour cards, number cards, die, enlarged 'blanked off' poem (see 'Preparation'), card, glue, scissors, coloured marker pens, Blu-tack, easel
- Duplicate sets of animal cards and colour cards (see 'Preparation')
- Shoe box or similar, paint, paintbrushes, play dough, PVA glue and water in 1:3 proportions, glue brushes

Optional materials for other activities

- Large building blocks to make a Number Five bus. Animal masks (optional)
- Variety of paints, including the primary colours, water, mixing trays, brushes

Preparation

- ▲ Enlarge the poem (p. 36) or type it on a computer using 24-point Tahoma with 1.5 spacing, then print it out. Fix the poem to the easel. Place the flip-chart beside the easel.
- ▲ Prepare the paints as required for the masks for Group A.
- ▲ Prepare red, blue, white and black paint, and paper for Group B.
- ▲ Enlarge the 'blanked off' poem on Photocopiable Sheet 5 (p. 38) and fix it to the easel. Make small balls of Blu-tack.
- ▲ Make two sets of animal cards and colour cards using Photocopiable Sheets 6 and 7 (pp. 39 and 40). You may want to put a 'splodge' of each colour on the colour cards, to help the children to read the word.

▲ Make a set of number cards and a die, coordinating the numbers on the die's faces with those on the number cards. You should use the numbers that the children know or are working on.

Introducing the poem

- Tell the children you're all going to share a nonsense poem – does anyone know what a nonsense poem is? Explain that they're usually funny because they don't make sense. Ask the children to listen carefully while you read the poem and afterwards they should try to decide why the poem is nonsense. Read the poem, tracking the text with your finger. When you have finished, ask the children to tell you which parts are nonsense (three purple elephants, a pink mouse, animals speaking, inviting the animals into the house, telling animals to catch a bus). See if they can identify which parts are true (a black and white panda, a yellow wooden house, opening the door to the house). Did they enjoy the poem? Can they say why or why not?
- Recite the poem again, this time encouraging the children to join in when they can. Use different voices for the various speakers in the poem – a high voice for the child and a deep voice for the elephants. Encourage the children to do the same.
- Tell the children you'd like them to help you make up some actions to go with the poem. Spend some time looking at each line and deciding what would express it appropriately. You could use Figure 3.1 as a stimulus if the children are really stuck for ideas. If not, draw their suggestions on the flip-chart and then agree a final version. Practise the new actions for a few minutes before reciting the poem together again, this time putting the actions to the words.
- Have a bit of fun changing the animals to make up a new poem, orally. Remind the children that the poem doesn't have to rhyme and it can be nonsense. For example,

> There were three purple hedgehogs,
> A little pink dog,
> A black and white zebra,
> A yellow wooden house.
>
> I opened the door
> Of my yellow wooden house,
> Said, 'Come inside, zebra.
> Come inside, dog.'
>
> The three purple hedgehogs said,
> 'What about us?'
> 'I'm sorry but you'll have to get
> The Number Five bus.'

Focus activities

Group A: Help the children to make masks (see Figure 3.2) of an elephant, a mouse and/or a panda. They could use their masks for imaginative play and/or when they are reciting *Three Purple Elephants*.

Group B: Let the children experiment with colours to discover how to make purple and pink. Help them to mix different colours until they discover that red and blue make purple, and red and white make pink. Let them paint the elephants, the mouse and the panda using their mixed colours. They could write a label, caption and/or sentence(s) for their pictures.

Group C: Give the children the animal cards, the colour cards, the number cards and the die. Show them the enlarged 'blanked off' version of the poem. Help them to play a game where they pick a card from each pile and then roll the die. They should then substitute the animals, the colours and the numbers by fixing the cards to the blank spaces with Blutack, and have fun reciting their new poem.

Group D: Give the children the duplicate sets of animal cards and/or the colour cards, according to achievement level. Let the children play snap, matching or pelmanism, as you (or they) wish.

Group E: Help the children to make models of an elephant, a mouse and a panda (see Figure 3.3), using play dough. Once they have finished, let the children paint their models in the colours featured in *Three Purple Elephants*. When the models are dry, varnish them with the PVA-water mixture and leave them to dry and harden off. Paint the shoe box yellow and make a model of a house for the animals.

Other structured play activities

- Arrange a visit to an animal park or zoo that has elephants among its residents.
- Turn the Home Corner into the Number Five bus and let the children role-play the purple elephants catching it and going on a journey (there may well be more elephants than the three of the poem!). They could make elephant masks and wear them (see Figure 3.2) as part of the imaginative play.
- Let the children explore freely with colours or paints in water, to discover what mixtures create what colours. For example, give them yellow and blue to discover how to make green, or let them try red and yellow to make orange, and so on. What will happen if they mix all the colours together?
- Put a selection of books about elephants, mice and pandas in the Library Corner and leave them for the children to explore freely in their own time. Put some beanbags or big cushions on the floor to give the children a relaxing experience.

Figure 3.1 Some actions to go with *Three Purple Elephants*

1. Elephant mask

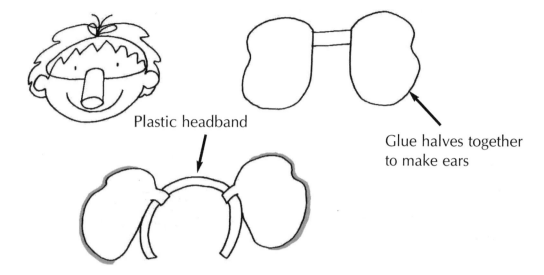

Plastic headband

Glue halves together
to make ears

2. Mouse mask

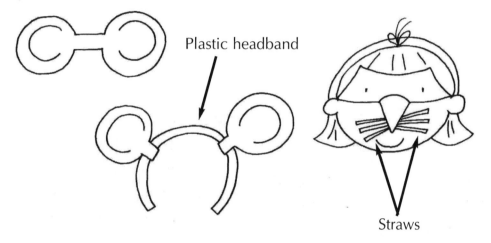

Plastic headband

Straws

3. Panda mask

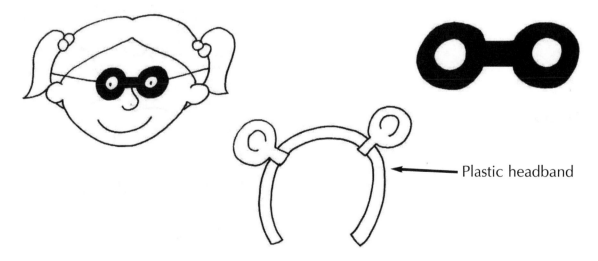

Plastic headband

Figure 3.2 Help the children to make these masks as part of exploring *Three Purple Elephants*

Use balls of play dough for the animals' bodies. Pinch out the ears from the ball of dough. Push whole cloves into the dough for eyes.

Elephant

Push in white straws for tusks, macaroni for the legs and feet and penne for the trunk. When the dough is hard, paint the model grey.

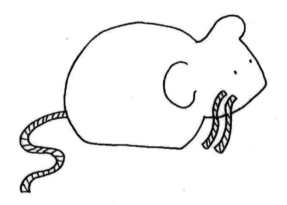

Mouse

Pinch the head into a mouse shape and flatten the base of the body. After painting, stick on strands of wool for the whiskers and tail.

Panda

Flatten the base of the body. Use white to paint the torso and the face, except the eyes, ears and nose. Paint the rest of the body black.

Figure 3.3 Help the children to make animal models using play dough

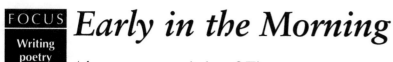

Early in the Morning

(Anonymous) (p. 37)

Early learning goals from *Curriculum guidance for the foundation stage,* Communication, language and literacy:

- Explore and experiment with sounds, words and texts.
- Use their phonic knowledge to write simple regular words and make phonically plausible attempts at more complex words.

Objectives from the *National Literacy Strategy (YR)*:

- To think about and discuss what they intend to write, ahead of writing it.
- To use experience of…poems…as a basis for independent writing, e.g. retelling, substitution, extension, and through shared composition with adults.

Materials needed

- Enlarged copy of *Early in the Morning* (see 'Preparation'), easel, Blu-tack
- Flip-chart and marker pens
- Enlarged copy of *Later in the Evening* (see 'Preparation')
- Enlarged copy of *Early in the Morning* without the sound words (see 'Preparation')
- Thin cork coasters, matchboxes or other small boxes, paint, glue, scissors, straws, water play tray
- Vehicle cards (see 'Preparation'), cassette recorder, blank cassette, paper and pencils
- Templates of aeroplane (see 'Preparation'), card, scissors, paint, string

Optional materials for other activities

- Cassette of environmental sounds, cassette recorder, blank cassette

Preparation

- ▲ Enlarge *Early in the Morning* (p. 37) and then fix it to the easel.
- ▲ Type *Later in the Evening* on the computer using 20-point Tahoma with double spacing, then print it out. Fix it to the easel and cover it up:

Later in the Evening

Come down to the station later in the evening,
See all the railway trains moving in a row.
See all the drivers closing down the engines,
Clickety click and clackety clack,
Back in they go!

Come down to the garage ·······································,
See all the buses moving in a row.
See all the drivers closing down the engines,
Rumble, rumble, rumble, rumble,
Back in they go!

Come down to the seaside ···························,
See all the motor-boats ··············· in a row.
See all the drivers closing down the engines,
Splishing, splishing, sploshing, sploshing,
Back in they go!

Come down to the airport ······························ ,
See all the aeroplanes ························· in a row.
See all the pilots ····················· the engines,
Whirring, whirring, whirring, whirring,
Back in they go!

▲ Blank out the sound words in a copy of *Early in the Morning* (i.e. the fourth line of each verse) and make an enlarged copy, leaving the spaces to be filled.
▲ Make a set of vehicle cards using Photocopiable Sheet 8 (p. 41).
▲ Make aeroplane templates as shown in Figure 3.5 on card. Make enough for each child in Group D.

Introducing the poem

- Ask the children to tell you what sort of vehicles we can travel in and list their ideas on the flip-chart. If they have said trains, buses, planes and boats, draw a circle around these on the list. Otherwise, add them to the list yourself. Tell the children you're all going to share a poem about these vehicles.

- Read the poem to the children, encouraging them to join in where they can and tracking the words with your finger as you recite. Use the first reading to let the children become aware of the poem's pattern and to learn the chant of the last line in each verse, then do a second reading to enable them to join in more.

- When you have finished the two readings, ask the children whether they like the poem. Can they say why or why not? Which is their favourite verse? Why? Can they tell you any nonsense words that are in the poem? For example, 'Clickety click' or 'splishing'. Ask them what these words are being used for, even if they aren't 'real' words. Explain that sometimes words like this are very useful for showing us noises and sounds. Have a look at the words in each verse that are used to show the noise made by the different vehicles. Point to each one and help the children to work out the phoneme blends. Do they think these 'sound words' are good? Can they say why or why not?

- Have a bit of fun inventing other nonsense sound words that the children think are good descriptions of the vehicles' noises. (At this stage, don't expand on the concept of onomatopoeia, since this is addressed later in the *National Literacy Strategy*.) Then spend some time learning the original sound words in each verse, to help the children join in with enthusiasm when you share the poem again.

- Look at the enlarged sheet with *Later in the Evening* and tell the children you're all going to make up a poem similar to *Early in the Morning* but it's about the end of the day, when all the vehicles are brought back for the night. Read the first verse together, encouraging the children to join in where they can. Ask them to help you put a word in the space in the second verse – they should think about the pattern of the first verse to help them. Write on the sheet what the children suggest, which is likely to be 'later in the evening'. Work through the poem in this way with the children, encouraging them to suggest words or phrases for the missing parts.

- When you have completed the poem together, share it a couple of times, letting the children enjoy the achievement of writing their own poem. They could also make up some actions to go with it.

Focus activities

Group A:　Look at the sheet with *Early in the Morning* minus its sound words. Have some fun with the children making up some new sound words for each of the vehicles. For example, the trains might go 'ta ta ta tum', the buses might go ' grum grum grum grum', the motor-boats might go 'frishing frishing froshing froshing' and the aeroplanes might go 'zumming zumming zumming zumming'. Encourage the children to try writing their new words phonetically. Explain that their words aren't 'real' words so they needn't worry about getting the spellings right!

Group B:　Help the children to make some models of motor-boats using the cork coasters and small boxes. Paint the matchbox with a door and windows, to make a cabin. Cut the coaster into a flat hull (see Figure 3.4) and stick the matchbox cabin onto it with glue. Make a hole in the cabin and push a straw through for a mast. Turn the water play area into a harbour and let the children float their boats. They could write a label, caption and/or sentence(s) about the harbour, according to achievement level.

Group C:　Give the paper, pencils, cassette recorder and the blank cassette to the children and put the vehicle cards face down on the table. Let the children play a game where they turn over a card and then experiment with different sounds and noises for the vehicle shown on the card. When they have decided on a sound word or noise, they should record it onto the cassette – remind them to say 'This is a . . . ' before they record the sound. Encourage them to write their new words, using their knowledge of phonemes. When they have made their 'package', leave it out for other children to read, listen to and practise writing the new words.

Group D:　Give each child an aeroplane template (see Figure 3.5) and help them to make a plane. Tell them they're going to make a joint 'air display'. Paint and cut out the sections before assembling them to make a simple plane. Thread a different length of string through each plane before hanging them all from the ceiling.

Group E:　Turn the Home Corner into a train. Help the children to make the timetables, the tickets, the destinations, the buffet menu and so on. Let them have free sessions of imaginative play, going on a journey.

Other structured play activities

- Record *Early in the Morning* onto a cassette so that the children can listen to it at leisure in an area of the room where they can relax. Also leave out a cassette of environmental sounds for the children to listen to. If the cassette has accompanying literature at the children's reading level, leave it there too.
- Take the children outside to listen to the sounds made by the different vehicles moving around in the local area. If possible, record some of them onto a cassette so that the children can listen to them again later. Have some fun making up words that express the vehicles' sounds.
- Let the children use Small People Play to make an airport, a harbour and/or a street, with the vehicles featured in *Early in the Morning*.
- Arrange a visit to an airport, a bus depot, a railway station and/or a harbour so that the children can experience the vehicles at first hand.

Make a flat 'hull' from the coaster, like this:

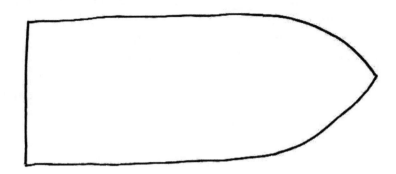

Stick the matchbox onto it for the cabin, like this:

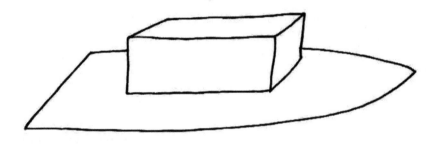

Make a hole in the matchbox for a
straw mast, like this:

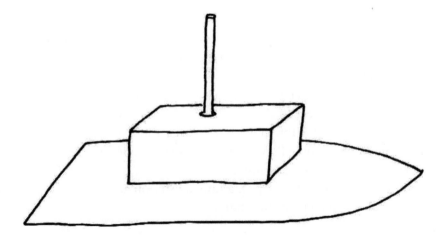

Figure 3.4 Help the children to make a coaster boat like this

To make an aeroplane, draw and cut out templates as shown in A, B and C. Cut slits in A (see dotted lines). Slide C through the front slit and B through the back.

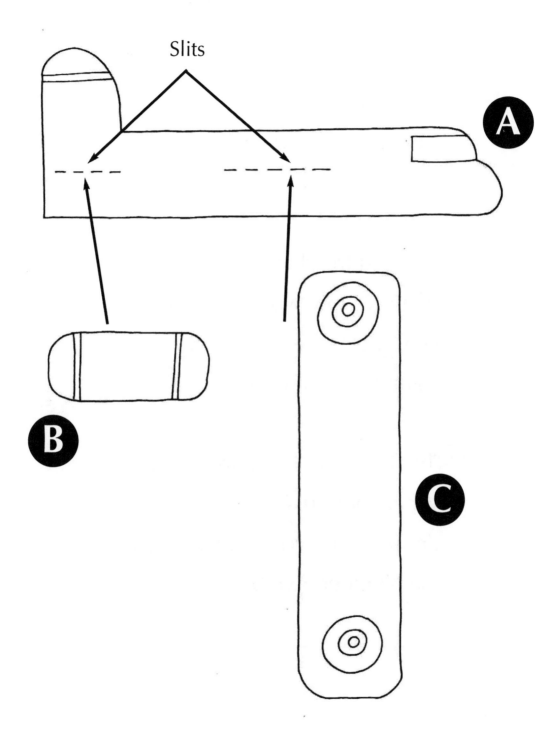

Figure 3.5 Help the children to make a simple aeroplane like this

Three Purple Elephants

Joan Poulson

There were three purple elephants,

A little pink mouse,

A black and white panda,

A yellow wooden house.

I opened the door

Of my yellow wooden house,

Said, 'Come inside, panda.

Come inside, mouse.'

The three purple elephants said,

'What about us?'

'I'm sorry but you'll have to get

The Number Five bus.'

Early in the Morning

Anonymous

Come down to the station early in the morning,
See all the railway trains standing in a row.
See all the drivers starting up the engines,
Clickety click and clackety clack,
Off they go!

Come down to the garage early in the morning,
See all the buses standing in a row.
See all the drivers starting up the engines,
Rumble, rumble, rumble, rumble,
Off they go!

Come down to the seaside early in the morning,
See all the motor-boats floating in a row.
See all the drivers starting up the engines,
Splishing, splishing, sploshing, sploshing,
Off they go!

Come down to the airport early in the morning,
See all the aeroplanes standing in a row.
See all the pilots starting up the engines,
Whirring, whirring, whirring, whirring,
Off they go!

There were ....,

A little ....,

A .... and ....,

A yellow wooden house.

I opened the door

Of my yellow wooden house,

Said, 'Come inside, ...

Come inside, ...'

The .... said,

'What about us?'

'I'm sorry but you'll have to get

The Number Five bus.'

giraffe

tiger

snake

monkey

ostrich

panda

blue	orange
green	red
brown	yellow

bus

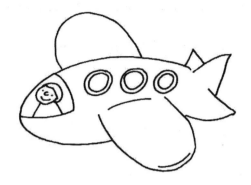

plane

boat

train

motor bike

bicycle

CHAPTER 4

Look at your hat!

by Barbara Ireson (p. 48)

Early learning goals from *Curriculum guidance for the foundation stage*, Communication, language and literacy:

- Enjoy listening to and using spoken and written language, and readily turn to it in their play and learning.
- Read a range of familiar and common words and simple sentences independently.

Objectives from the *National Literacy Strategy (YR)*:

- To read on sight a range of familiar words.
- To reread and recite...rhymes with predictable and repeated patterns and experiment with similar rhyming patterns.

Objectives from the *National Literacy Strategy (Y1)*:

- To read familiar...poems independently, to point while reading and make correspondence between words said and read.
- To recite...rhymes with predictable and repeating patterns, extemporising on patterns orally by substituting words and phrases, extending patterns, inventing patterns and playing with rhyme.

Materials needed

- ■ Enlarged copy of *Look at your hat!* (see 'Preparation')
- ■ Cassette recorder/player, blank cassette
- ■ Clothes cards (see 'Preparation'), card, scissors, glue, a feely bag, plastic alphabet letters *h, s, d, c, t* and *j*, plus others if more cards are required (see 'Preparation')
- ■ A selection of clothes in duplicate, for example two socks, two cardigans, two baseball caps, two shoes, etc., a large bag or sack, word cards for the articles of clothing (optional)
- ■ Clothes cards (see 'Preparation')
- ■ Selection of clothes (including a hat, a shirt, a dress and a pair of shoes), a clothes line, pegs, paper and pencils or marker pens

Optional materials for other activities

- ■ 'Sight recognition' word cards, as required
- ■ A hat and/or a shoe

Preparation

▲ Enlarge *Look at your hat!* on a photocopier or by typing it on a computer in 24-point Tahoma with 1.5 line spacing, then print it out.

▲ Record *Look at your hat!* on the blank cassette, leaving out the item of clothing at the end of lines one, two and five (for example, 'Look at your…!/Just look at your…!/It's back to front/And squashed quite flat./Look at your…!'). Make sure you recite the poem slowly enough for the children both to follow and join in. Put the cassette in the player ready to play.

▲ Make two sets of clothes cards using Photocopiable Sheet 9 on p. 50 (for Groups B and D). If you want more cards, you could stick pictures of clothes from magazines onto card; make sure the initial letters of these extra cards are put into the feely bag for Group B.

▲ Put one of each of the duplicate clothes into the large bag or sack. Make a set of word cards to match each article of clothing (optional).

Introducing the poem

• Tell the children you're all going to share a poem about children who are scruffy. Can the children tell you when they are scruffy themselves? For example, at the end of a session of rough and tumble, or when they've been outside playing all day. Discuss the ways in which they might be scruffy – their tee-shirt may be dirty, their trainers scratched or the knees of their trousers torn.

• Share the poem with the children, tracking the words with your finger and encouraging them to join in. Use intonation and expression to put across the sense of outrage being felt by the speaker. When you have finished, ask the children whether they enjoyed the poem. Can they tell you why or why not? Do they think it's a funny poem? Do they feel sorry for the children in the poem, or do they think the speaker is just making a fuss?

• Look at the text in a little more detail. Are there any words or phrases that the children aren't sure of? For example, what does 'And needs a press' mean? What would the dress look like if it's 'rumpled and crumpled'? Why are the shoes 'full of holes'? What does 'What a disgrace!' mean? Explore each verse and ask the children to suggest how the clothes got into that state. For example, how did the hat become squashed and back to front, or how did the shoes become full of holes? Why do the children in the poem have to go home? Have some fun together thinking of different scenarios that could have resulted in this 'scruffiness'.

• Divide the children into three groups and allocate the first, second and final lines of the first verse to each group. Help them to practise speaking their lines for a few minutes and then put them together to recite the complete verse, with you speaking the third and fourth lines. When the children are confident, you could help them to perform the rest of the poem in this way, ending with everyone shouting *GO HOME*.

• Have a bit of fun substituting some of the clothes mentioned in *Look at your hat!*, reminding them that their poem doesn't have to rhyme. For example,

Look at your trousers!	Look at your trainers!
Just look at your trousers!	Just look at your trainers!
They're rumpled and crumpled	They're full of holes –
And need a press.	Not fit to use.
Look at your trousers!	Look at your trainers!

Focus activities

Group A: Give the cassette player and the cassette recording of the poem to the children. Let them listen to it, joining in with the poem and adding the missing words. They could follow the text on the enlarged version for support.

Group B: Put the clothes cards face up on the table. Let the children play a game where they take a letter from the feely bag, say its phoneme and then find a picture of an item of clothing that begins with the letter. If they're correct, they win a token; the child with the highest number of tokens at the end of the game is the winner.

Group C: Using the sack containing half of the duplicate clothes, play a game where you show the children an article of clothing and ask them one by one to feel inside the sack until they find it. They should then identify the word card to match their article if you have opted for this part of the game.

Group D: Put the clothes cards face down on the table. Have some fun with the children using the repeated pattern of *Look at your hat!* Let the children take turns to pick a card and identify the article of clothing before substituting it in a verse of the poem. For example, 'Look at your jumper!/Just look at your jumper!/It's back to front/And squashed quite flat./Look at your jumper!' According to achievement level, they could write one of their new verses using the enlarged version for support.

Group E: Help the children to put up the clothes-line and peg the clothes onto it. Ask them to put the hat, shirt, dress and shoes in the order they appear in the poem. Help the children to write labels, captions and/or sentence(s) about the items hanging on the line.

Other structured play activities

- Use a hat and/or a shoe to hold 'sight recognition' word cards that you'd like the children to learn. Let them take turns to pick out a card and read the word. The high frequency words that appear in *Look at your hat!* are *look, at, it, and, a, of, to* (YR), *your, just, back, out, black, not, been* and *what* (Y1–2). You could add a bit of extra fun by letting them win tokens for correct recognition.
- Help the children to make a collage of the child(ren) in the poem, using fabric for the clothes. Draw around one of the children for the outline(s), and then 'dress' the figure(s) to look scruffy. The children could write labels, captions, sentence(s) or parts of the poem to go with the collage.
- Make a big clothes scrapbook together. Let the children find pictures of articles of clothing to go into the book. Help them to write labels or captions for each page. Leave the book in the Story Corner for the children to explore in their own time.

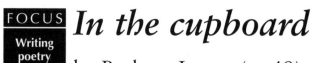

In the cupboard

by Barbara Ireson (p. 49)

Early learning goals from *Curriculum guidance for the foundation stage,* Communication, language and literacy:

- Use talk to organise, sequence and clarify thinking, ideas, feelings and events.
- Use their phonic knowledge to write simple regular words and make phonetically plausible attempts at more complex words.

Objectives from the *National Literacy Strategy (YR)*:

- To apply knowledge of letter/sound correspondences in helping the teacher to scribe, and rereading what the class has written.
- To use experience of ... poems as a basis for independent writing ...

Objectives from the *National Literacy Strategy (Y1)*:

- Through shared and guided writing to apply phonological, graphic knowledge and sight vocabulary to spell words accurately.
- To use rhymes ... as models for their own writing.

Materials needed

- ■ Enlarged copy of *In the cupboard* (see 'Preparation'), sheet of paper large enough to cover all the poem except the first two lines, easel, Blu-tack
- ■ Flip-chart and marker pens
- ■ Two enlarged copies of *In the cupboard* with the fruit words blanked out (see 'Preparation')
- ■ Thick paper or thin card to make zigzag books (see 'Preparation'), coloured marker pens, magazines, scissors and glue (optional)
- ■ Two sets of number cards (for Groups B and C) and two sets of fruit cards (for Groups B and D) (see 'Preparation')
- ■ Plastic or magnetic numerals and board

Optional materials for other activities

- ■ Materials for a frieze
- ■ Large carton for a model cupboard, play dough, paint, paintbrushes
- ■ Real fruit as featured in the poem (according to season and availability)

Preparation

▲ Type *In the cupboard* on a computer using 24-point Tahoma, leaving out the fruit words, then print out two copies, one for the whole-group session and one for Group E. Fix one copy to the easel.

▲ Enlarge *In the cupboard* (p. 49) on a photocopier or type it on a computer using 24-point Tahoma, then print it out. Fix it to the easel on top of the blanked-out version and then cover all of it up except for the first two lines, with the paper. Put the flip-chart beside the easel.

▲ Make zigzag books by cutting a strip of thick paper long enough to make sufficient 'pages', to accommodate the children's own version of *In the cupboard*. Fold the paper in concertina style, making sure the pages are equal in size.

▲ Make a set of cards, each one showing a number word from one to ten; use Photocopiable Sheets 10 and 11 (pp. 51 and 52) to make two sets of cards, each showing a picture and/or word (as required), of one of the fruits in *In the cupboard*. (One set for Group B and one for Group D.)

Introducing the poem

• Ask the children to help you read the title of the poem. Can they guess what it might be about? Together, read the first two lines and then have a bit of fun guessing what might be in the cupboard. Jot down some of the children's ideas on the flip-chart. Uncover the rest of the poem except for the last line, and read it with the children, encouraging them to join in. Pause before the last line and ask the children to guess what's up on the shelf. Make the reading of the last line dramatic so that the children can enjoy the surprise. Had they guessed about the birthday cake? Did they enjoy the poem? Can they say why or why not? Were they surprised that there was fruit in the cupboard?

• Remove the enlarged copy of *In the cupboard* and show the children the blanked-out version underneath. Explain to them that you'd like some help to write a new poem, in the style of *In the cupboard*. Read through the unfinished poem together and ask the children what they would like to have in their version. Jot their ideas on the flip-chart. They may suggest, for example, animals, monsters or vehicles, or they may decide not to have a category as such, preferring to choose different things on each line. Encourage them to think of something for the end that will give the reader a big surprise. Brainstorm some ideas, jotting these down on the flip-chart.

• Spend a bit of time discussing the final choice and then complete the unfinished poem by filling in the spaces. According to achievement level, the children could write the words, or you may have to scribe for them. Have some fun reading through and reciting the new poem together. Encourage them to use expression and intonation to make their poem sound interesting and exciting.

Focus activities

Group A: Give the zigzag books to the children and help them to write their new version of *In the cupboard*. Put each of the numbered items on a separate page. If you're using objects that can be found in a magazine, let the children cut out the pictures and stick them onto the appropriate pages, otherwise let them illustrate their books.

Group B: Give the number and fruit cards to the children. Encourage them to play with the number and fruit words to make new lines for the poem. For example, they might put together 'six' and 'oranges' instead of 'six plums' as in the original. Challenge them to discover the one fruit that can't be changed (lemon) and why (because it's in the singular). (They could, of course, add 's' onto 'lemon' and take it off the substitute.) According to achievement level, they could write their new lines.

Group C: Give the children a set of number cards and ask them to put them in order. Help them to think of things with the same initial phoneme as each number. For example, 'two trees/turtles/toffees', 'three thumbs/thimbles/thistles' or 'nine nettles/nuts/necklaces'. Watch out for 'one' – the sound at the beginning of the word needs to be 'w' as in 'wish' not 'o'.

Group D: Give the children a set of fruit cards and the plastic or magnetic numerals and board. Let them have fun matching the numerals to the fruit, using the enlarged copy of the poem for support if they wish.

Group E: Let the children choose a category such as vegetables, animals, clothes and so on. Help them to list ten things within their category. For example, for clothes they might think of coat, shirt, jumper, hat, socks, trousers, pyjamas, scarf, cardigan and gloves. According to achievement level, help them to substitute their list in the poem, using a copy of the blanked-out version.

Other structured play activities

- Go to the supermarket with the children and buy some of the fruit featured in *In the cupboard*, if possible the number of each as in the rhyme. Let the children eat the fruit at snack time, reminding them to wash their hands first. (Make sure none of them is allergic to any of the fruit.) Talk about the fruit in terms of colour, size, shape, smell, taste and so on. You could also arrange a visit to a 'pick your own' fruit farm if the season is right.
- Make a frieze of two giant cupboards, one filled with the fruit and the birthday cake from *In the cupboard* and the other with the things from the children's new poem. The children could write labels, captions and/or sentence(s) for the frieze.
- Make the fruits in the poem from play dough, painting them the correct colours when they're dry. Help the children to make a model birthday cake and using the large box, make a cupboard with two or three shelves for all the goodies.
- Turn a cupboard in the Home Corner into the cupboard in the poem, using plastic fruit and a model birthday cake. Let the children role-play and recite the poem.

Look at your hat!

Barbara Ireson

Look at your hat!
Just look at your hat!
It's back to front
And squashed quite flat.
Look at your hat!

Look at your shirt!
Just look at your shirt!
It's inside out
And black with dirt.
Look at your shirt!

Look at your dress!
Just look at your dress!
It's rumpled and crumpled
And needs a press.
Look at your dress!

Look at your shoes!
Just look at your shoes!
They're full of holes –
Not fit to use.
Look at your shoes!

Look at your face!
Just look at your face!
It hasn't been washed
What a disgrace!
Look at your face!

GO HOME

In the cupboard

Barbara Ireson

I went to the cupboard
And what did I see?

One lemon
Two oranges
Three apples
Four pears
Five peaches
Six plums
Seven bananas
Eight cherries
Nine gooseberries
Ten raspberries . . .

And up on the shelf
All by itself –
A BIRTHDAY CAKE FOR ME!

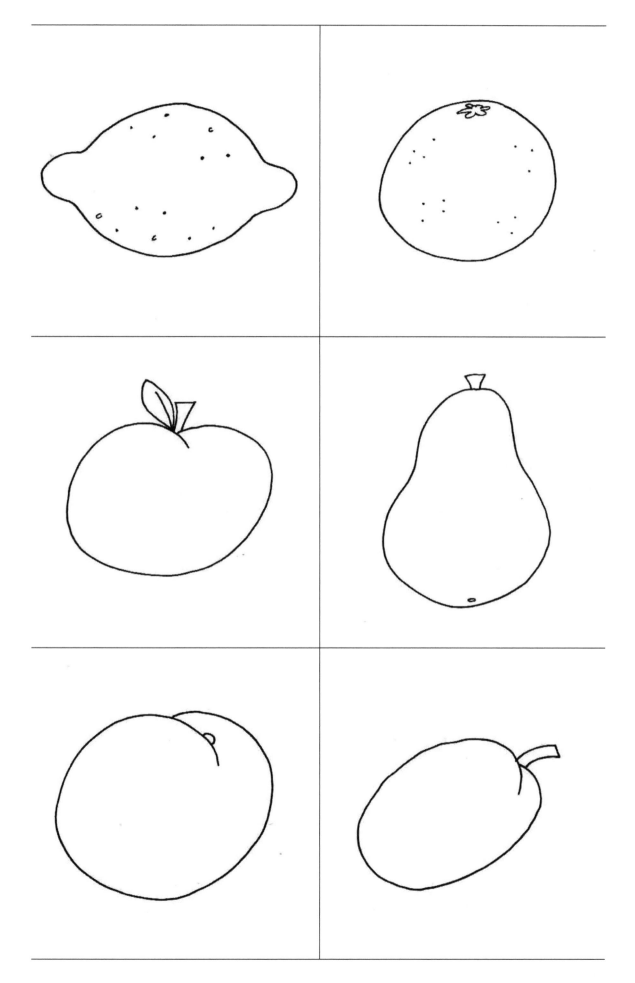

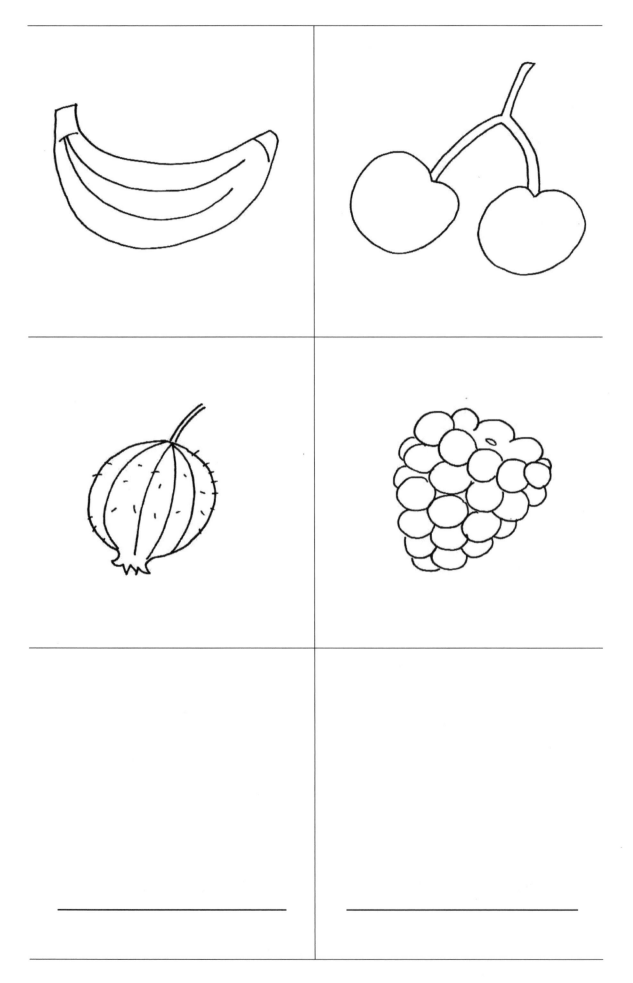

CHAPTER 5

When I Get Up in the Morning
by Clive Webster (p.60)

Early learning goals from *Curriculum guidance for the foundation stage,* Communication, language and literacy:

- Use language to imagine and recreate roles and experiences.
- Explore and experiment with sounds, words and texts.

Objectives from the *National Literacy Strategy (YR)*:

- To use knowledge of familiar texts to re-enact or retell to others, recounting the main points in the correct sequence.
- To understand and be able to rhyme through extending rhyming patterns by analogy, generating new and invented words in speech and spelling.

Objectives from the *National Literacy Strategy (Y1)*:

- From YR, to practise and secure the ability to rhyme, and relate this to spelling patterns through generating rhyming strings.
- To recite . . . rhymes with predictable and repeating patterns, extemporising on patterns orally by substituting words and phrases, extending patterns, inventing patterns and playing with rhyme.

Materials needed

- ■ Enlarged copy of *When I Get Up in the Morning* (see 'Preparation')
- ■ Easel and Blu-tack
- ■ Flip-chart and marker pens
- ■ Copy of Figure 5.1 (optional; see 'Preparation')
- ■ Rhyming word/picture cards (see 'Preparation'), card, glue, scissors, tokens
- ■ Plastic alphabet letters, including enough to make at least three sets of 'ed', 'at' and 'en' endings, feely bags, trays
- ■ Snakes and ladders board, tiddlywinks, word/picture cards (see 'Preparation')
- ■ Pyjamas and/or nightdress, face-cloth, soap, toothbrush, toothpaste, hairbrush, cereal bowl and spoon
- ■ Getting Up cards (see 'Preparation')
- ■ Picture/word cards (see 'Preparation')

Optional materials for other activities

- ■ Roll of wallpaper, marker pens
- ■ Selection of action rhyme anthologies (see 'Other structured play activities')
- ■ A4 sheets divided into quarters, coloured marker pens or crayons, pencils and paper if required
- ■ The children's own pyjamas, toothbrush, toothpaste and hairbrush

Preparation

▲ Enlarge *When I Get Up in the Morning* (p. 60) on a photocopier or type it on a computer using 18-point Tahoma, then print it out. Fix the copy to the easel. Put the flip-chart beside the easel.

▲ Make a set of rhyming word/picture cards using Photocopiable Sheet 12 (p. 62). Put the plastic alphabet letters 'ed', 'at' and 'en' into the three trays to make rhyming families; put a starter word in each tray, for example 'bed', 'cat' and 'pen'; put the remaining plastic alphabet letters into the feely bag.

▲ Make a set of Getting Up cards using Photocopiable Sheet 13 (p. 63). Stick the sheet on card and cut it into the individual cards.

▲ Make a set of word/picture cards using Photocopiable Sheet 14 (p. 64). Stick the sheet on card and cut it into the individual cards.

Introducing the poem

• Ask the children to read the title of the poem with you, tracking the words with your finger as you read. Has anyone an idea of what the poem might be about? What do the children do when they get up in the morning? Jot a key word and/or picture for each thing they tell you. Help them to keep their routine in sequence. For example, they should say 'I eat breakfast' after 'I get up'. (Unless of course they have breakfast served in bed every morning!)

• Share the poem with the children, using the first reading to let them become familiar with its content. When you have finished, see whether the children's routines talked about at the beginning of the session are similar to the one in Clive Webster's poem. Spend a moment or two discussing any differences. For example, some children may clean their teeth *after* breakfast.

• Read the poem again, encouraging the children to join in with you. Have a bit of fun by pausing before the last word of each verse and letting the children supply it. During the next reading, you could encourage the children to supply the word at the end of the second line of each verse – they will be more familiar with the poem by this stage and should be able to predict the missing word. See if the children can identify the rhyming words in each verse (bed/head; face/place; teeth/underneath; hair/everywhere; tummy/yummy).

• Tell the children you want them to help you make up some actions to go with the poem. Look at the first verse and together decide on some actions that would express 'stretch and yawn' and 'scratch my sleepy head'. When you have all decided, make a sketch on the flip-chart to help the children remember the actions when they recite the poem again. Work through each of the remaining four verses until the children have made up actions for the whole poem. Alternatively, use the actions suggested in Figure 5.1 either as they stand or to give the children some ideas for their own actions.

• Have some fun reciting the poem together again, this time adding all the actions. When the children are confident, divide them into four groups and allocate one line of each verse to each group, i.e. Group 1 takes all the first lines, Group 2 has all the second lines and so on. You might need to practise a bit first, so the children get the idea of reciting 'in the round'. Perform the poem once more, this time letting each group speak its lines in turn, while every-one does the actions.

Focus activities

Group A: Ask the children to sort the rhyming word/picture cards into the rhyming families. Play a game where the children take turns to add another word to one of the families.

The word can be nonsense or sensible, as long as it rhymes. For example, if the child adds to the 'bed/head/shed' family, they could say 'red/said/ ged/pred' and so on. If the child's word rhymes with the family, they win a token. The child with the highest number of tokens at the end of the game is the winner.

Group B: Give the rhyming family trays and the feely bag containing the plastic alphabet letters to the children. Let them take turns to pick a letter from the feely bag and make a new word for one of the rhyming families. Let them make a nonsense word, as long as they can tell you what it says and it is a true rhyme that fits into the family.

Group C: Play a game using the snakes and ladders board and the word/picture cards. Put the cards face down on the table and ask the children to take turns to pick a card and read the word written on it (the picture will support the children who need a bit of help). If the child can suggest a word in the same rhyming family, they move their tiddly-wink to the bottom of the next snake or ladder and go up it. Nonsense words are allowed, as long as they are in the rhyming family. The child who reaches the top first is the winner. (Ignore snakes' heads – the tiddlywinks always travel upwards.)

Group D: Give the children the props from the poem (pyjamas and/or nightdress, face-cloth, soap, toothbrush, toothpaste, hairbrush, cereal bowl and spoon). Encourage them to sort the props into the order they appear in the poem. Let them recite the poem with you, using the props to perform the actions they made up during the first session.

Group E: Give the Getting Up cards to the children and ask them to put them into the correct sequence, as shown in the poem. If you're sure the children have a good concept of sequencing, let them have fun putting the cards out of order and role-playing the result. For example, eating their breakfast and then having to get back into bed in order to tumble out of it.

Other structured play activities

- Make some life-size pictures (draw outlines of the children on the back of a roll of wallpaper), each one showing the child doing an action from one verse of the poem. Ask the children to help you order the pictures before pinning them along the wall.
- Have fun exploring other action poems together. Some stimulating collections are *First Verses*, compiled by John Foster (Oxford University Press 1996), *Playtime Rhymes for Little People*, compiled by Mary Finch and illustrated by Clare Beaton (Barefoot Books 2001) and for rhymes with a musical dimension, try *Bobby Shaftoe, clap your hands* by Sue Nicholls (A & C Black 2001).
- Help the children to make a musical accompaniment to *When I Get Up in the Morning*. Let them choose the instruments and experiment with sounds and rhythms to accompany the poem when it is being recited.
- Ask the children to make a picture sequence in cartoon-style of their own getting-up routine at home, using the quartered A4 sheets. Help them to select four key elements and draw each one in a section of the paper. They could write a label, caption and/or sentence(s) to go with their cartoon.
- Have fun role-playing the poem by letting the children dress up in their own pyjamas and perform the getting-up routine in reality. If possible, do this shortly before snack time, so that the children can have 'breakfast' as well.

Figure 5.1 Some actions to go with *When I Get Up in the Morning*

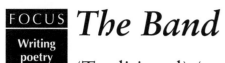

The Band

(Traditional) (p. 61)

Early learning goals from *Curriculum guidance for the foundation stage*, Communication, language and literacy:

- Explore and experiment with sounds, words and texts.
- Use their phonic knowledge to write simple regular words and make phonetically plausible attempts at more complex words.

Objectives from the *National Literacy Strategy (YR)*:

- To learn new words from reading and shared experiences...
- To apply knowledge of letter/sound correspondences in helping the teacher to scribe, and rereading what the class has written.

Objectives from the *National Literacy Strategy (Y1)*:

- Through shared and guided reading to apply phonological, graphic knowledge and sight vocabulary to spell words accurately.
- To use rhymes...as models for their own writing.

Materials needed

- Enlarged copy of *The Band* (see 'Preparation'), easel, Blu-tack
- Flip-chart and marker pens
- Enlarged copy of unfinished extra verses (see 'Preparation')
- Picture or poster of an orchestra
- A selection of musical instruments, cassette recorder/player, blank cassette
- Instrument cards (see 'Preparation'), card, glue, scissors
- Copies of Photocopiable Sheet 16 (see 'Preparation'), scissors, paper, glue, pencils or markers
- Junk to make instruments

Optional materials for other activities

- More copies of the unfinished extra verses of *The Band* (Photocopiable Sheet 15)
- A selection of musical instruments

Preparation

- ▲ Enlarge the unfinished extra verses of *The Band* (Photocopiable Sheet 15 on p. 65) on a photocopier. Fix the sheet to the easel and put the easel beside the flip-chart.
- ▲ Enlarge *The Band* (p. 61) on a photocopier or type it on a computer using 20-point Tahoma, then print it out. Fix it over the unfinished verses already on the easel.
- ▲ Make two sets of instrument cards using Photocopiable Sheet 16 (p. 66). You could write the name of each instrument if required.
- ▲ Make enough copies of Photocopiable Sheet 16 for each child in Group C.

Introducing the poem

- Look at the picture of an orchestra or band and discuss with the children what some of the instruments look like. Does anyone know what they sound like? Read the title of *The Band* together and ask the children to guess what the poem is about. Share the poem, encouraging the children to join in. When you have finished, ask the children whether they enjoyed the poem. Can they say why or why not? Ask the children to look at the picture of the orchestra and point to the instruments that are in the poem.

- Look at the poem again and ask the children to think of some actions that could go with each verse. For example, they could imitate playing each instrument. Practise the actions you all decide on and then recite the poem together again, doing the actions at the right places. Can the children suggest some other musical instruments that could be used for the poem? Have another look at the poster if they need a few ideas. What actions could they perform to show these instruments? Can they make up some words to show what the instruments sound like? For example, a guitar might go 'twang'. Jot down some of the children's ideas on the flip-chart and together decide on two new instruments and the words for their sounds.

- Uncover the unfinished verses under the copy of *The Band* and read them with the children. Ask the children to help you transfer the words that they decided on for their new verses, to the spaces on the sheet. Together recite the new verses, performing the actions at the same time. Add them to the original poem and have a lively, action recital of the whole work. You could add some real instruments to the performance for a bit of extra zest!

Focus activities

Group A: Give the instruments, cassette recorder and blank cassette to the children. Let them explore the instruments and help them to make up words that describe what the instruments sound like. Record the children playing an instrument and then saying the onomatopoeic word they made up. According to achievement level, they could write their words phonetically. Leave the recorder, cassette and instruments out to enable the other children to explore Group A's activity.

Group B: Put the instrument cards face down on the table. Play a game where the children take turns to pick a card. They should identify the instrument, perform an action to show how it's played and say a word to show how it sounds. If they need a bit of support in this part, let them look at the poem to jog their memories.

Group C: Give each child a copy of Photocopiable Sheet 16, paper, scissors and glue. Ask the children to cut out the instruments carefully and glue them onto the paper. Help them to write a label, caption and/or sentence(s) on their collages. Can they write a sound word for each instrument as well?

Group D: Make some junk instruments with the children and let them have fun trying to play them. For example, fill different containers with water, dried pulses, pasta and so on before tapping them with different 'knockers' or shaking them; use cardboard boxes or empty crisp or biscuit cylinders as drums and hang metal spoons from different lengths of string before hitting them with a metal clapper. (Make sure none of the children is allergic to any of the foods that were originally in the containers.) Can they make up words to describe how their new instruments sound?

Group E: Help the children to discover how they can use their own bodies as instruments to make music. For example, clapping, snapping fingers, humming, 'popping' their forefinger from their lips, whistling, 'zzzzzzz'ing and so on. Encourage them to compose a piece of music together and help them to write down their work, using symbols and/or words.

Other structured play activities

- Have fun with the children, setting *The Band* to music. Let them make up their own composition and accompany themselves as they recite the poem. You could split the children into players and speakers, changing over to give everyone a turn at both parts.
- Help the children to make up even more verses to *The Band* using other instruments as the stimulus. Make more copies of the unfinished verses (Photocopiable Sheet 15 on p. 65) and help the children to write their new words in the blank spaces. Have a gala performance of the whole poem when the children are happy with their work.
- Persuade your local secondary school orchestra to play for the children. (You'll know best who should visit whose setting.) Let the children experience the instruments at first hand and, if possible, have a go at playing some of them.
- Leave the instruments out for the children to explore freely in their own time. Encourage them to work in pairs or groups and compose some music themselves. They could notate their work by drawing symbols for each instrument played.

When I Get Up in the Morning
Clive Webster

When I get up in the morning
I tumble out of bed,
I yawn and stretch and stretch and yawn
And scratch my sleepy head.

When I get up in the morning
I always wash my face,
And splash and splash the soapy water
All around the place.

When I get up in the morning
I always clean my teeth,
Front and back and back and front,
On top and underneath.

When I get up in the morning
I always brush my hair,
Brush it this way, brush it that,
Brush it everywhere.

When I get up in the morning
I always rub my tummy,
Because I know my breakfast's waiting –
Yummy, yummy, yummy.

The Band
Traditional

We can play on the big bass drum,
And this is the music to it:
Boom – boom – boom goes the big bass drum,
And that's the way we do it!

We can play on the violin,
And this is the music to it:
Zing – zing – zing goes the violin,
And that's the way we do it!

We can play on the saxophone,
And this is the music to it:
Soo – soo – soo goes the saxophone,
And that's the way we do it!

We can play on the tambourine,
And this is the music to it:
Tink – tink – tink goes the tambourine,
And that's the way we do it!

bed	head	face
race	hair	bear
shed	space	pear

hat

pen

tin

cot

fan

bun

tap

peg

cup

The Band

We can play on the ....,

And this is the music to it:

.... goes the ....,

And that's the way we do it!

We can play on the ....,

And this is the music to it:

.... goes the ....,

And that's the way we do it!

CHAPTER 6

Sing a Song of Sixpence

(Traditional) (p. 74)

Early learning goals from *Curriculum guidance for the foundation stage*, Communication, language and literacy:

- Enjoy listening to and using spoken and written language, and readily turning to it in their play and learning.
- Listen with enjoyment, and respond to ... songs ... rhymes and poems ...

Objectives from the *National Literacy Strategy (YR)*:

- To understand and be able to rhyme through recognising, exploring and working with rhyming patterns.
- To use knowledge of rhyme to identify families of rhyming CVC words.

Objectives from the *National Literacy Strategy (Y1)*:

- From YR, to practise and secure the ability to rhyme, and to relate this to spelling patterns through ... generating rhyming strings.
- To blend phonemes to read CVC words in rhyming and non-rhyming sets.

Materials needed

- Enlarged copy of *Sing a Song of Sixpence* (see 'Preparation'), easel, Blu-tack, six pence (real money), if possible some rye and/or rye bread
- Bread, butter or spread, honey, knives, plates, etc., aprons
- Black paint, paintbrushes, white paper, pencils or marker pens, scissors, glue, blackbird template (see 'Preparation'), words or spellings as required (see 'Focus activity' for Group B)
- A clothes peg, a model pie (plastic from the Home Corner, or a play dough version), a hat and a toy cup
- Enlarged copy of *Sing a Song of Sixpence* minus the rhyming words (see 'Preparation'), sticky notes with a rhyming word written on each, easel
- Ingredients for pastry (see 'Preparation'), aprons, cooking utensils as required

Optional materials for other activities

- Rye bread, butter or spread, knives, aprons
- Materials and equipment to make an imaginative play area
- Picture of a blackbird, general book about garden birds

Preparation

▲ Enlarge *Sing a Song of Sixpence* (p. 74) on a photocopier or type it on a computer in 24-point Tahoma, then print it out. Fix it to the easel.

▲ Prepare the relevant work area for food preparation.

▲ Find a picture of a blackbird and make blackbird templates for each child in Group B.

▲ Make a copy of *Sing a Song of Sixpence*, leaving out the rhyming words (rye/pie; sing/King; money/honey; clothes/nose and again/seen) by typing it on a computer in 24-point Tahoma and printing it out. Write one rhyming word from the poem on each sticky note. Fix the poem to the easel and place the mixed sticky notes down the side(s).

▲ Collect the ingredients for the pastry recipe in Figure 6.1 (p. 70).

Introducing the poem

• Show the money to the children and ask them how much it is. Explain that our money long ago was called pounds and pennies (i.e. not pence) and that six pence would have bought many more things than now. We used to say *sixpence* (put the emphasis on the 'six') as one word, or *ninepence* or *thruppence* (three pence). Can the children think of any poems that have 'sixpence' in them? Read the title of *Sing a Song of Sixpence* together and then recite the rhyme, encouraging the children to join in. Track the text with your finger as you go through it. Let the children sing it if they'd rather.

• Did the children already know the nursery rhyme? Do they like it? Why or why not? Are there any words or phrases in it that they aren't sure of? For example what do *rye, dainty dish, counting-house, parlour* and *seam* mean? If you have some rye and/or rye bread, show it to the children and talk about it; explain that rye is a bit like wheat and can be used to make flour for baking. Can the children tell you another way of saying *four and twenty*? How would we say *thirty-two* or *sixty-eight* in the old way? (*Two and thirty* and *eight and sixty.*)

• Explore the text in more detail. Are there any rhyming words? See if they can tell you what they are (rye/pie; sing/King; money/honey). According to achievement level, you could explain that *clothes/nose* and *again/seen* are half rhymes or near rhymes. Do the children think the rhyme could be true? Which parts are nonsense? For example, baking twenty-four singing blackbirds in a pie, the maid's nose being pecked off by a blackbird and the King's doctor sewing it on again. Enjoy reciting or singing the rhyme together again. You could divide the children into groups and give each one a verse, before all coming together again for the final verse.

Focus activities

Group A: Together prepare some bread and butter or spread for snack time. Help the children to put some honey on the bread. Remind them to wash their hands first. Make sure none of them is allergic to wheaten products, the butter/spread or the honey. Help them to use a knife carefully and correctly.

Group B: Help the children to make a mobile with blackbirds and then write a label, caption and/or sentence(s) about it. They could make twenty birds and write one line of each verse on a bird. Alternatively, they could use the birds to practise writing, reading and spelling their current word list by putting one word on each bird.

Group C: Give the clothes peg, model pie, hat and toy cup to the children and play a game where they hold one of the objects and make a rhyming string by saying a word. Everyone should agree that the word rhymes before the object is passed on.

Nonsense words are allowed and words can be repeated. If any children want to 'pass', let them do so without any pressure and they can join in when they're more confident.

Group D:　Ask the children to help you place the sticky notes with the rhyming words in the right places on the poem. Read the poem together and let the children decide which word is missing and which sticky note needs to be put there.

Group E:　Help the children to make some pastry and shape the dough into bird shapes (see recipe in Figure 6.1). Remind them to wash their hands first. If they're going to eat their blackbirds, make sure none of them is allergic to wheaten products.

Other structured play activities

- Let the children taste rye bread at snack time. You can buy it at most good supermarkets or in a delicatessen. Put butter or spread on it. Remind the children to wash their hands first. Make sure none of them is allergic to rye products or the butter/spread. Help them to use a knife carefully and correctly.

- Use large equipment to make a '*Sing a Song of Sixpence* play area' outside. Use benches or dividers to make a counting house and a parlour; create a separate 'garden' with a clothes line; make a kitchen area for baking the pie. Collect or make props such as money, the pie, bread and honey, pegs, basket and laundry, and the doctor's instruments. Let the children make a role-play or have imaginative play sessions. You could also create this indoors using the Home Corner.

- Spend some time together watching for the blackbirds in the setting's playground. Have a picture of a blackbird handy that the children can use for identification. Talk about the size, shape and colour of the birds (male and female are different), about their yellow beaks and their song. Talk about some of the other birds that you see at the same time.

Pastry Blackbirds

Ingredients

450g plain flour   100g sugar
100g butter or margarine   Cold water to mix
100g lard   whole cloves

Method

Preheat the oven to 200°C or Gas Mark 6. Rub the butter or margarine into the flour until it resembles breadcrumbs. Add the sugar and mix. Make a well in the centre of the mixture and add the water, gradually mixing it to form a soft dough. Make birds by rolling a small piece of dough into a ball for the body, make a smaller ball for the head and attach it to the body using a small quantity of cold water. Pinch out a beak on the front of the head. Put a clove on each side of the head for eyes. Bake in the preheated oven for about 20 minutes or until golden brown. Cool before eating.

Figure 6.1 How to make pastry blackbirds

Planting Beans

(Traditional) (p. 75)

Early learning goals from *Curriculum guidance for the foundation stage*, Communication, language and literacy:

- Interact with others, negotiating plans and activities and taking turns in conversation.
- Listen with enjoyment to ... rhymes and poems and make up their own ... rhymes and poems.

Objectives from the *National Literacy Strategy (YR)*:

- To reread and recite stories and rhymes with predictable and repeated patterns and experiment with similar rhyming patterns.
- To think about and discuss what they intend to write, ahead of writing it.

Objectives from the *National Literacy Strategy (Y1)*:

- To learn and recite simple poems and rhymes, with actions, and to reread them from the text.
- To use rhymes ... as models for their own writing.

Materials needed

- ■ Enlarged copy of *Planting Beans* (see 'Preparation'), enlarged copy of Photocopiable Sheet 17 (see 'Preparation'), easel, Blu-tack, flip-chart, marker pens
- ■ Enlarged copy of Photocopiable Sheet 18 (see 'Preparation')
- ■ Green sugar paper for bean leaves (see 'Preparation'), white paper, glue, scissors, pencils
- ■ Body parts cards (see 'Preparation'), feely bag, arrows (see 'Preparation'), thick black card, scissors, marker pens
- ■ Dried beans, different containers

Optional materials for other activities

- ■ Clear plastic empty water/juice bottles; blotting paper; broad bean seeds; absorbent paper or paper kitchen-towels; water
- ■ Selection of beans

Preparation

- ▲ Enlarge Photocopiable Sheets 17 and 18 (pp. 76 and 77) or type them on a computer in 26-point Tahoma, then print them out. You could add more verses to the unfinished version(s) if you wish.
- ▲ Enlarge *Planting Beans* (p. 75) or type it on a computer in 26-point Tahoma, then print it out.

▲ Fix the enlarged Photocopiable Sheet 17 to the easel, then fix *Planting Beans* on top of it. Put the easel beside the flip-chart.

▲ Make large bean leaves using green paper.

▲ Make a set of cards, each with the name and/or a picture of a body part as required; put the cards into the feely bag; make each child an arrow from thick black card.

▲ Collect the bread, butter or spread, baked beans and cooking utensils for making beans on toast, aprons.

Introducing the poem

• Tell the children you're going to share a rhyme about planting beans; ask them to join in. Can anyone read the title? Read it together, tracking the words with your finger. Share the rhyme with the children, pausing at rhyming words to let them guess the word – you could give them a clue by telling them it rhymes. For example,

> Here we plant our beans in a row,
> Do you know, do you know?
> Here we plant our beans in a . . .
> In the garden where they. . .

As you read the following verses, the children should pick up the pattern and join in with you.

• Ask the children to help you make up some actions to go with each verse. Jot down a key word or a small drawing on the flip-chart for each idea the children come up with. Have some fun experimenting with their suggestions until you have all decided on the final versions. Recite the rhyme together again, performing the actions at the same time.

• Uncover the enlarged version of Photocopiable Sheet 17 and tell the children you want them to help you write some more verses for the rhyme. Together read the text of the unfinished rhyme and then brainstorm some ideas for completing the verses. For example, they might suggest *knee*, *thumb*, *chin* or *ear*. When you have all made a final choice, fill in the spaces – according to achievement level, the children could write the words or you could scribe for them. Then decide on some actions to go with the new verses. Recite the rhyme together once more, adding the new verses and actions.

Focus activities

Group A: Use *Planting Beans* as a model to write a new rhyme together. Look at the enlarged version of Photocopiable Sheet 18 and decide on something different to grow and a different way of planting it. Help the children to draft and redraft their ideas and then write the final version of their new rhyme.

Group B: Help the children to make a beanstalk going up the wall, using the green sugar paper for the stalk and the leaves. Have fun finding words to rhyme with *row* and *beans*, including nonsense words, and write them on pieces of white paper. Stick the words to the leaves to make a 'rhyming beanstalk'.

Group C: Give each child an arrow. Play a game where the children take turns to pick a body part card from the feely bag and hold it up. (According to achievement level, they could also read the word aloud.) The first child to point with his or her arrow to the right body part takes out the next card.

Group D: Make some beans on toast for snack time. Help the children to list what they need for the session and discuss the preparation sequence. Remind them to wash their hands and wear their aprons. Make sure none of the children are allergic to any of the ingredients.

Group E: Let the children make some shakers with the dried beans and containers. Help them to explore how to make different sounds and pitches using the different types and sizes of container, as well as different quantities of beans inside.

Other structured play activities

- Grow some beans. Soak the broad bean seeds overnight in water. Cut the bottoms off the plastic water/juice bottles, to a height of about 15 cm (don't use glass jars for safety reasons), line them with the blotting paper and fill the centre hole with the absorbent paper or paper kitchen-towels. Place the broad bean seeds between the blotting paper and the bottle so that the children can see them easily. Pour in enough water to make sure the blotting paper and the centre paper are wet – keep the containers well watered. Put them in a warm place out of direct sunlight and don't allow them to dry out. The children will begin to see some results in a few days. Help the children to label and write captions for their beans.

- Make a 'Beans collection' including baked beans, runner beans, broad beans, dried beans, haricot beans and kidney beans. Let the children explore them freely. They could write labels, captions and/or sentence(s) about the display.

- Put *Planting Beans* to music (see Figure 6.2). If you can't read music yourself, ask someone who can to record the simple tune onto a cassette so that you and the children can learn it. Then let the children play some instruments to accompany themselves as they sing the poem/song.

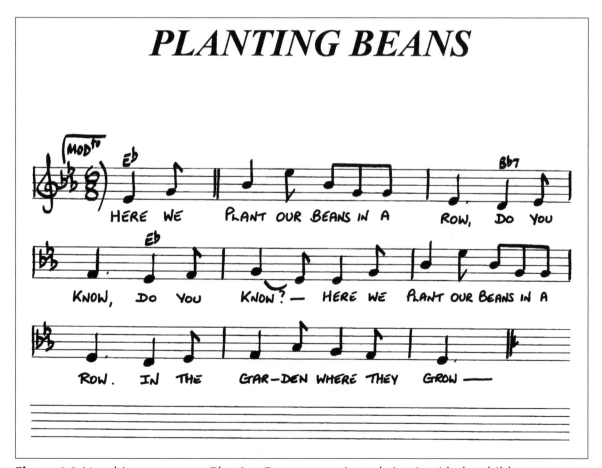

Figure 6.2 Use this tune to put *Planting Beans* to music and sing it with the children

Sing a Song of Sixpence
Traditional

Sing a song of sixpence,
A pocket full of rye;
Four and twenty blackbirds
Baked in a pie.

When the pie was opened
The birds began to sing;
Wasn't that a dainty dish
To set before the King.

The King was in his counting-house
Counting out his money;
The Queen was in the parlour
Eating bread and honey.

The maid was in the garden
Hanging out the clothes,
When down came a blackbird
And pecked off her nose.

They sent for the King's doctor
Who sewed it on again.
He sewed it on so neatly
The seam was never seen.

Planting Beans

Traditional

Here we plant our beans in a row,
Do you know, do you know?
Here we plant our beans in a row,
In the garden where they grow.

With our toe we plant them so,
Do you know, do you know?
With our toe we plant them so,
In the garden where they grow.

With our heel we plant them so,
Do you know, do you know?
With our heel we plant them so,
In the garden where they grow.

With our hands we plant them so,
Do you know, do you know?
With our hands we plant them so,
In the garden where they grow.

With our nose we plant them so,
Do you know, do you know?
With our nose we plant them so,
In the garden where they grow.

With our .... we plant them so,

Do you know, do you know?

With our .... we plant them so,

In the garden where they grow.

With our .... we plant them so,

Do you know, do you know?

With our .... we plant them so,

In the garden where they grow.

Here we plant our .... in a row,

Do you know, do you know?

Here we plant our .... in a row,

In the garden where they grow.

With our .... we plant them so,

Do you know, do you know?

With our .... we plant them so,

In the garden where they grow.

CHAPTER 7

New Shoes

(Anonymous) (p. 85)

Early learning goals from *Curriculum guidance for the foundation stage*, Communication, language and literacy:

- Listen with enjoyment, and respond to ... rhymes and poems ...
- Explore and experiment with sounds, words and texts.

Objectives from the *National Literacy Strategy (YR)*:

- To reread and recite ... rhymes with predictable and repeated patterns and experiment with similar rhyming patterns.
- To identify ... the initial and dominant phonemes in spoken words.

Objectives from the *National Literacy Strategy (Y1)*:

- To recite ... rhymes with predictable and repeated patterns ...
- From YR, to practise and secure the ability to rhyme ... through exploring and playing with rhyming patterns.

Objectives from the *National Literacy Strategy (Y2)*:

- To identify and discuss patterns of rhythm, rhyme and other features of sound in different poems.
- To discriminate, orally, syllables in multi-syllabic words using children's names and words from their reading.

Materials needed

- ■ Enlarged copy of *New Shoes* (see 'Preparation'), easel, Blu-tack
- ■ Old shoes from the dressing-up box, paint, paint trays, paper
- ■ Word cards (see 'Preparation'), die (see 'Preparation' if a 'tailor made' die is required)
- ■ The children's own name cards, a set of general name cards (see 'Preparation')
- ■ Musical instruments to express 'squeaky', 'shiny', 'creaky' and 'leaky' – let the children help you to choose which ones
- ■ 'Footwear' and 'wearer' cards (see 'Preparation')

Optional materials for other activities

- ■ Shoes from the dressing-up box, string, scissors
- ■ A variety of shoes such as a football boot, a ballet shoe, a baby's shoe, a lady's trainer, a man's slipper and so on
- ■ Materials to make a centipede frieze

Preparation

▲ Enlarge *New Shoes* (p. 85) on a photocopier or type it on a computer using 24-point Tahoma, then print a copy. Fix it to the easel and cover it.

▲ Mix the paint to a consistency thick enough for printing with the soles of the old shoes. Pour the paint into the paint trays.

▲ Make a set of word cards using Photocopiable Sheet 19 (p. 87). Make a die, putting the number on each face as you require.

▲ Use Photocopiable Sheet 20 (p. 88) to make a set of name cards.

▲ Make a set of 'wearer' and 'footwear' cards using Photocopiable Sheets 21 and 22 (pp. 89 and 90).

Introducing the poem

• Ask the children whether any of them are wearing new shoes – do they like them? Why or why not? Does everyone like having new shoes? Why or why not? Are they allowed to choose the shoes when they go to buy them? Tell them you're all going to share a poem about new shoes.

• Uncover the poem and ask the children to help you read the title. Share the poem, tracking the words with your finger as you read. Encourage the children to join in when they can. When you have finished reading, ask the children whether they enjoyed the poem. Can they tell you why or why not? Explain that it's fine not to like a poem or a story.

• Can the children identify who is speaking in the poem? How do they know it's a child? Can they tell whether it's a boy or a girl? Do they think it matters? Have they ever felt the same way as the child in the poem? If not about shoes, then maybe about something else, such as a jumper or a coat. Can they explain why the child in the poem liked his or her old shoes so much? Why does the child dislike the new shoes so much?

• Explore the text in a little more detail. Ask the children what the main rhyming family in the poem is ('squeaky', 'creaky' and 'leaky'). Have a bit of fun making up some nonsense words to rhyme with the '–eaky' family. For example, 'teaky', 'gleaky' and 'preaky'. See if the children can identify another, smaller rhyme ('away' and 'today').

• What do the children notice about the ends of the first three lines in each verse? Do they like the repetition of the word 'shoes'? Can they tell you why or why not? Share the poem once more, encouraging the children to join in as you read aloud.

Focus activities

Group A: Help the children to make prints using the soles of the old shoes from the dressing-up box: dip the sole of the shoe into the paint and carefully place it on the paper to make a print. The children could write a label, caption or sentence(s) to explain about their prints. Make a display.

Group B: Give the die to the children and place the word cards face down on the table. Let the children play a game where they turn over two cards and read the words before deciding whether they belong to the same rhyming family. If their answer (either 'Yes' or 'No') is correct, they should roll the die for a score for that answer. The winner is the child with the highest score at the end of the game. You may need to keep the children's scores for them.

Group C: Give the children their name cards and put on the table the name cards you made. Help the children to work out the syllables in their own names by clapping together as you say each name. Work out which names in the group have two syllables. Clap the words 'squeaky', 'creaky' and 'leaky' and help the children work out that these words also have two syllables. Look at the name cards you made and help the children to work out which ones have the same number of syllables as 'squeaky', 'creaky' and 'leaky'. You may have to read some of the names to the children.

Group D: Help the children to make a musical accompaniment to *New Shoes*. They should practise playing their instruments as they recite the words 'squeaky', 'shiny', 'creaky' and 'leaky'. Be prepared for a bit of noise – you might prefer to do this activity away from the main working room! When the children are confident enough, let them give a performance of their recitation for the others.

Group E: Put the 'wearer' and 'footwear' cards on the table (facing up or down, according to how you want the game to be played). Let the children play a game where they have to match the footwear to the wearer. For example, the football boots to the football player. You could play this as Pelmanism or straightforward matching.

Other structured play activities

- Arrange a visit to a shoe shop. Ask the assistants to show the children the foot measuring gauges, the shoe boxes, the footstools, shoehorns and so on.
- Help the children to make a hanging display of the shoes from the dressing-up box, by tying different lengths of string around them and suspending them from the ceiling.
- Play a game with the selection of shoes where the children have to decide who would wear each shoe. Have a bit of fun making up where the person would wear the shoe and where they would *not* wear it. For example, the football player would wear the boot on the pitch but not in the bath.
- Make a giant centipede frieze and let the children put on its pairs of feet as many different types of shoe or footwear as they can. Let them look at the footwear section of a catalogue for some ideas if they need a bit of support. They could make the shoes by cutting out the pictures from the catalogue and sticking them onto the centipede, or by painting or drawing them on.

FOCUS
Writing
poetry

I Don't Like Custard

by Michael Rosen (p. 86)

Early learning goals from *Curriculum guidance for the foundation stage*, Communication, language and literacy:

• Listen with enjoyment, and respond to...rhymes and poems and make up their own...rhymes and poems.
• Use their phonic knowledge to write simple regular words and make phonetically plausible attempts at more complex words.

Objectives from the *National Literacy Strategy (YR)*:

• To locate and read significant parts of the text, e.g. rhymes and chants.
• To use experience of...poems...as a basis for independent writing, e.g. retelling, substitution, extension, and through shared composition with adults.

Objectives from the *National Literacy Strategy (Y1)*:

• To recite stories and rhymes with predictable and repeating patterns, extemporising on patterns orally by substituting words and phrases, extending patterns, inventing patterns and playing with rhyme.
• To use rhymes and patterned stories as models for their own writing.

Objectives from the *National Literacy Strategy (Y2)*:

• To learn, reread and recite favourite poems, taking account of punctuation; to comment on aspects such as word combinations, sound patterns (such as rhymes, rhythms, alliterative patterns) and forms of presentation.
• To use simple poetry structures and to substitute own ideas, write new lines.

Materials needed

■ Enlarged version of *I Don't Like Custard* (see 'Preparation')
■ Easel and Blu-tack
■ Flip-chart and marker pens
■ Group poem *I Don't Like...* (see 'Preparation')
■ Food cards (see 'Preparation'), card, glue, scissors, cassette recorder/player and blank cassette or copies of *I Don't Like ...* and pens, as required
■ Ingredient cards (see 'Preparation'), feely bag
■ Plastic alphabet letters (your choice according to the phonemes being learnt), feely bag, tokens
■ Magazines with photos of food, paper, glue, scissors, pens, paper

Optional materials for other activities

■ Ingredients for real custard (see recipe in Figure 7.1 on p. 84), cooking utensils, children's aprons
■ Selection of poems with a food theme (see 'Other structured play activities')
■ Graph paper with large squares, coloured marker pens

Preparation

▲ Put the flip-chart beside the easel.
▲ Enlarge *I Don't Like Custard* (p. 86) on a photocopier and then fasten it to the easel and cover it up.
▲ Enlarge the group poem *I Don't Like...* (Photocopiable Sheet 23 on p. 91) or copy the poem onto a page of the flip-chart.
▲ Make some food cards by copying Photocopiable Sheet 24 (p. 92).
▲ Make a set of ingredient cards using Photocopiable Sheet 25 (p. 93) and put them into the feely bag.

Introducing the poem

• Spend a bit of time discussing with the children the foods they really dislike. Is there anything that seems to be disliked by most of the children? Encourage them to tell you why they don't like the food they talk about. Make a list of the food named by the children – let them write the list or scribe for them.
• Tell them you're all going to read a poem by Michael Rosen about custard and why he doesn't like it. Is custard on the children's list of foods they dislike? Uncover the poem and share it with the children. Try to use intonation, tempo and volume to express the moods in the poem. Encourage the children to join in with any words or phrases they can read. When you have finished reading, ask the children whether they enjoyed the poem. Can they tell you why or why not?
• Explore the text of the poem in a little more detail. What's the chant between each verse? ('I don't like custard', repeated.) Does the poem rhyme? How? Point out how the last word on lines two and four of each verse rhyme (or have a near-rhyme). Does the poem have a pattern? Show how the first two lines of each verse are always the same. For example, **'Sometimes it's** lumpy/**sometimes it's** thick', **'Don't want it on my** pie/**don't want it on my** cake' or **'It dribbles on the** table/**It dribbles on the** floor'.
• Share the poem once more, encouraging the children to join in where they can, especially with the chants. Then tell them you're all going to write a poem about food they don't like. Look at the list you wrote at the beginning of the session and together choose one food from it, to feature in your poem. Look at the copy of the group poem *I Don't Like...* that you prepared earlier on and tell the children you're all going to finish the poem by filling in the word spaces.
• Read the incomplete poem together, asking the children to think about what could go into the spaces to make a good poem. Brainstorm their ideas and write some key words on the flip-chart before making a final choice as a group. Remind the children that their poem doesn't have to rhyme. Complete the poem by asking the children to write their chosen words in the empty spaces, or by scribing for them. Here's an example of a completed poem:

I Don't Like Ice Cream

I don't like ice cream
I don't like ice cream

Sometimes it's pink
sometimes it's brown
It doesn't matter where I am
It always makes me frown

I don't like ice cream
I don't like ice cream

It's sticky in my fingers
It's sticky on the plate
It's sticky in my tummy
It's stuff I really hate

I don't like ice cream
I don't like ice cream

- Have some fun reciting the new poem together, encouraging the children to use gestures and facial expressions to show the mood of the poem.

Focus activities

Group A: Give the ingredient cards and the feely bag to the children. Let them play a game where they take two cards out of the feely bag and read them to make up a meal. For example, *slugs and chips* or *spiders and flies stew*. They could illustrate their meals and write a caption for their pictures. Let them role-play making their meals, using art and craft materials for the ingredients.

Group B: Give the group the feely bag containing the plastic alphabet letters and the tokens. Let them play a game where they pick a letter from the feely bag, read it and choose a food beginning with its phoneme. They should then say either 'I don't like...' or 'I love...', and if they're correct, they win a token. For example, if they take out 's', they could say, 'I don't like spinach' or 'I love sausages'. The winner is the child with the most tokens at the end of the game.

Group C: Let the children cut out from the magazines pictures of different food(s) they don't like and stick them onto paper. They should write a caption for their picture saying 'I don't like...'. You may need to help them with the spellings of some of the food.

Group D: Help the children to learn some or all of *I Don't Like Custard*, making up some actions and facial gestures to express the mood of the poem. If they find it difficult to learn a whole verse, help them to learn the chant and to join in with that when you have read each verse.

Group E: Put the food cards face down on the table and let the children play a game where they turn over a food card and together make up a poem in the style of *I Don't Like Custard*. Tell them their poem can be as funny or as yukky as they like. They could look at the group poem made up in the first session to help them if they need some support. Encourage them to record their poems onto the cassette or write them on their *I Don't Like...* sheets, according to achievement level and as you wish.

Other structured play activities

- Make some real custard with the children and let them have a taste (see Figure 7.1). Remind the children to wash their hands first, and wear their aprons. (Make sure none of the children is allergic to eggs or milk.) While they're eating the custard, read the poem to them again, making it as funny as possible for them.
- Share some other poems with the children about food. For example, John Foster's collection *Food Rhymes* (Oxford University Press 1998) has poems such as *When Susie's Eating Custard* (John Foster), *Beans* (Mike Jubb), *Gingerbread Man* (Celia Warren), *A Munching Monster* (Marian Swinger) and *When the Giant Comes to Breakfast* (John Coldwell).
- Visit the local supermarket and explore the kinds of food it sells that the children don't like. Make a list of their dislikes while you're there and use it as a memory-jogger when you get back to the setting. With the children, make a large block graph showing which foods they don't like and help the children to write the labels and captions for it.
- Ask the children to bring in empty packets from the foods they don't like and make a display. Help them to write labels, captions and/or sentence(s) about the display according to achievement level. You could also make a complementary display with empty packets of the children's *favourite* foods.

Custard Sauce

Ingredients

1 egg
300 ml milk
2–3 drops of vanilla essence

1 level dessertspoon of caster sugar
1 level dessertspoon of cornflour

Method

Beat the egg. Blend the cornflour with half of the cold milk. Boil the remaining milk, adding the cornflour mix and stirring until boiling. Cook for two or three minutes, allow to cool and then add the sugar, vanilla essence and beaten egg. Return to the boiling ring and stir until the egg thickens, but do not allow it to boil.

NOTE: MAKE SURE THE CUSTARD SAUCE IS VERY COOL BEFORE ALLOWING THE CHILDREN TO TASTE IT.

Figure 7.1 How to make real custard

New Shoes

Anonymous

My shoes are new and squeaky shoes,
They're very shiny, creaky shoes,
I wish I had my leaky shoes
That Mummy threw away.

I liked my old brown leaky shoes
Much better than these creaky shoes,
These shiny, creaky, squeaky shoes
I've got to wear today.

I Don't Like Custard

Michael Rosen

I don't like custard
I don't like custard

Sometimes it's lumpy
sometimes it's thick
I don't care what it's like
It always makes me sick

I don't like custard
I don't like custard

Don't want it on my pie
don't want it on my cake
don't want it on my pudding
don't want it on my plate

I don't like custard
I don't like custard

It dribbles on the table
It dribbles on the floor
It sticks to your fingers
Then it sticks to the door

I don't like custard
I don't like custard

I can't eat it slowly
I can't eat it quick
Any way I eat it
It always makes me sick

I don't like custard
I don't like custard

shoes	squeaky
shiny	creaky
Mummy	leaky
away	today
wear	wish
these	new
brown	better

Susan	Manjit
David	Jason
Michael	Leon
Harvinder	Stephanie
Ann	James
Philippa	Christina
Ben	Joseph

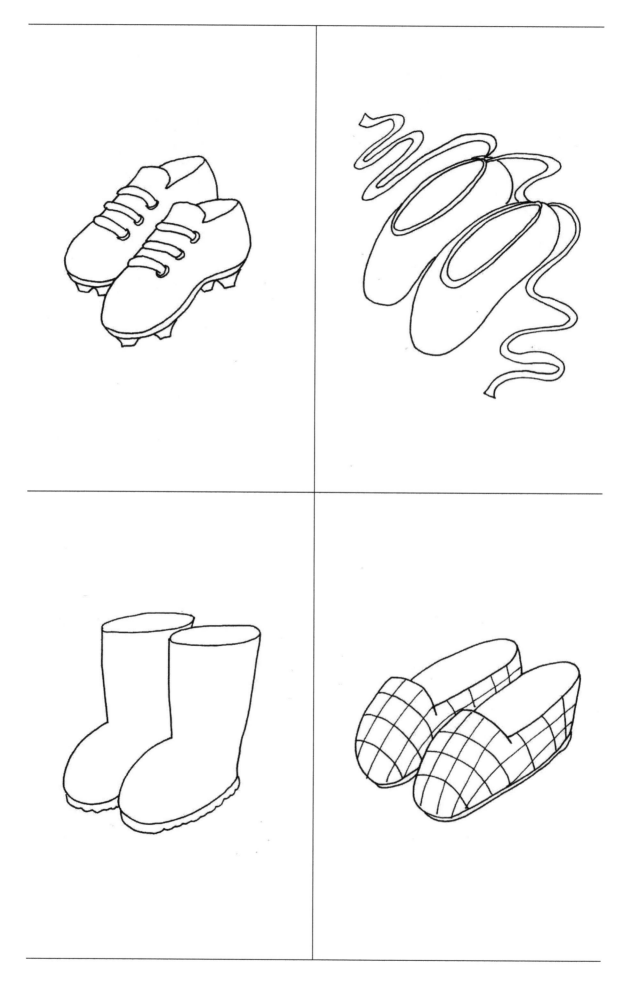

I Don't Like . . .

I don't like ....

I don't like ....

Sometimes it's ....

sometimes it's ....

It doesn't matter where I am

I don't like ....

I don't like ....

I don't like ....

It's .... in my fingers

It's .... on the plate

It's .... in my tummy

It's stuff I really hate

I don't like ....

I don't like ....

spaghetti

cabbage

jelly

beefburger

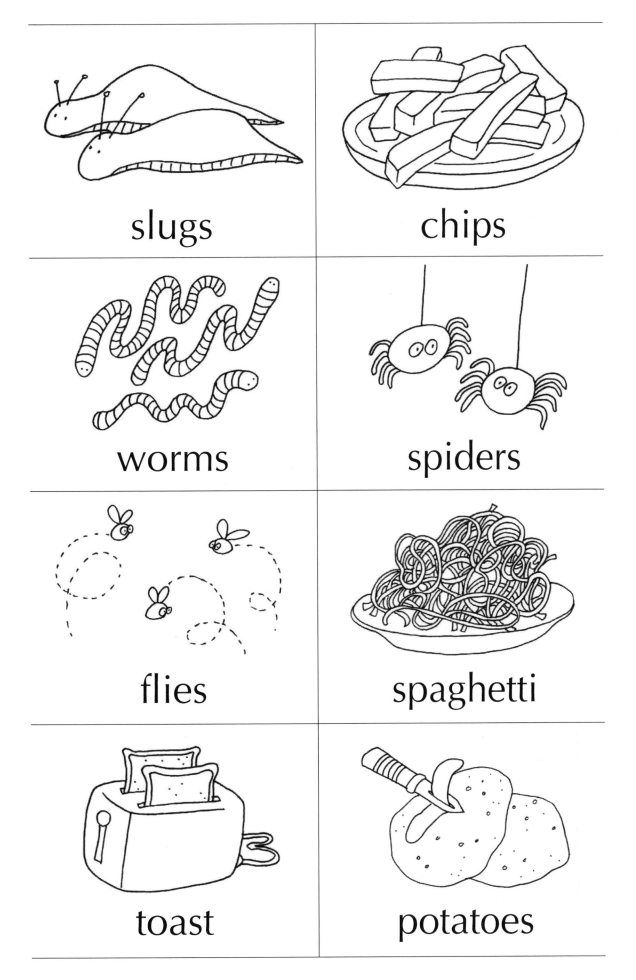

slugs

chips

worms

spiders

flies

spaghetti

toast

potatoes

CHAPTER 8

Cousin Peter

(Traditional) (p. 100)

Early learning goals from *Curriculum guidance for the foundation stage*, Communication, language and literacy:

- Interact with others, negotiating plans and activities and taking turns in conversation.
- Sustain attentive listening, responding to what they have heard by relevant comments, questions or actions.

Objectives from the *National Literacy Strategy (YR)*:

- To understand and be able to rhyme through recognising, exploring and working with rhyming patterns.
- To use knowledge of familiar texts to re-enact or retell to others, recounting the main points in the correct sequence.

Objectives from the *National Literacy Strategy (Y1)*:

- To retell stories, to give the main points in sequence...
- To learn and recite simple poems and rhymes, with actions, and to reread them from the text.

Objectives from the *National Literacy Strategy (Y2)*:

- To be aware of the difference between spoken and written language through comparing oral recounts with written text.
- To understand time and sequential relationships in stories.

Materials needed

- Enlarged copy of *Cousin Peter* (see 'Preparation'), easel, Blu-tack
- Flip-chart and marker pens
- Cassette recorder/player, blank cassette
- Draughtboard, draughtsmen, kick-off cards (see 'Preparation'), card, glue, scissors, feely bag
- Long strip of paper for each child in Group C, coloured marker pens, scrap paper, pencils
- A3 paper, paints, paintbrushes
- Action sequencing cards (see 'Preparation')

Optional materials for other activities

- Copy/copies of *Cousin Peter*, cassette recorder/player, blank cassette

Preparation

▲ Enlarge *Cousin Peter* (p. 100) on a photocopier or type it on a computer in 22-point Tahoma, then print it out. Fix it to the easel. Put the easel beside the flip-chart.

▲ Record the following instructions onto the blank cassette: *Knock three times upon the door, Wipe your feet upon the mat, Hang your hat upon the hook, Kick your shoes off one by one, Dance about in stockinged feet, Make a bow and say 'Goodbye'.*

▲ Leave enough space between each instruction to allow the children to switch the cassette player off and on again without losing the next instruction.

▲ Make a set of kick-off cards using Photocopiable Sheet 26 (p. 102). Put the cards into the feely bag.

▲ Put out A3 paper, paints and paintbrushes for Group D.

▲ Make some action sequencing cards: type the first line of each verse from *Cousin Peter* on a computer in 22-point Tahoma, then print it out, e.g. *He hung his hat upon the hook, He knocked three times upon the door* and so on.

Introducing the poem

• Ask the children whether anyone has a cousin called Peter. Tell them that you're all going to share a poem called *Cousin Peter* – point to the title – and that they'll soon be able to join in with you when they hear its pattern. Read the poem to the children, tracking the text with your finger, at a pace that allows them to link the spoken word with the written one. They should be able to pick up and join in with the repetitions of the first line of each verse fairly quickly.

• When you have finished, ask the children whether they enjoyed the poem. Why or why not? Which verse was their favourite? Why? Were there any words or phrases they didn't understand? For example, what does *He made a bow* ... mean? Recite the poem together again, but with some variations for a bit of fun. For example, you could read the first lines, they could read the second lines and you could all read the third and fourth lines together; or you could split everyone into three groups, each group saying a line and everyone saying the last line together; or split them into four groups where everyone says one line only.

• Ask the children to help you make up some actions to go with each verse in the poem. Brainstorm their ideas and jot down a few key words on the flip-chart. Experiment with some of the actions together and then make a final decision about which ones to perform. Practise the actions until the children are confident about what to do in each verse and then have fun performing the poem together again, adding the actions to the words as you all recite.

Focus activities

Group A: Give the cassette player and recorded cassette to the children. Ask them to listen to the instructions on the tape and then perform the actions. Tell them they should switch off the player while they're doing each action and then switch it back on again for the next instruction.

Group B: Put the draughtboard and each child's draughtsman on the table. Give the feely bag and the kick-off cards to the children. Let them take turns to pick a card, read it and then tell you a word that rhymes with the word on their card (nonsense words are allowed). For example, someone who picks *feet* could say *Sheet, heat* or *breet*. Whenever the children are correct, move their draughtsmen one space forward. The first child to reach the opposite side of the board is the winner.

Group C: Help the children to make a comic strip of *Cousin Peter*. Each picture should follow the sequence of the poem. Let them practise and change their ideas on the scrap paper before putting their final versions onto the long strips of paper. You could make one, group comic strip rather than individual ones, if this is more appropriate.

Group D: Help the children to make up some more things that Cousin Peter could do. For example, *He put his coat upon the chair, He took a brush and brushed his hair* or *He put on a scarf to keep him warm*. Let the children paint pictures on A3 paper to illustrate the new actions. They could write labels, captions and/or sentence(s) to go with their paintings.

Group E: Give the action sequencing cards to the children and ask them to put them in the right order. Let them refer to the enlarged copy of the poem if they need a bit of support. If you're sure their concept of sequencing is sound, they could play about with the sentences to make a nonsense version of *Cousin Peter*, which is arranged out of order.

Other structured play activities

- Use the poem to support number work by changing the number of times Cousin Peter knocked upon the door, when you're reciting the poem together. Use the numbers that the children are currently working on.
- Record the poem onto a cassette and leave the text and the cassette player with the recorded cassette ready to play in the Book Corner for the children to listen to, read and recite in their own time.
- Personalise the poem by substituting the children's own names for Cousin Peter (e.g. 'Last evening Cousin Jamie came' or 'Last evening Cousin Chloe came').
- Let the children role-play the poem in the Home Corner. Remind them to keep to the sequence of Cousin Peter's actions. Let them check against the enlarged copy to jog their memories if they need a bit of support.

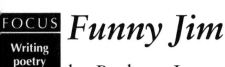

Funny Jim

by Barbara Ireson and Christopher Rowe (p. 101)

Early learning goals from *Curriculum guidance for the foundation stage*, Communication, language and literacy:

- Link sounds to letters, naming and sounding the letters of the alphabet.
- Explore and experiment with sounds, words and texts.

Objectives from the *National Literacy Strategy (YR)*:

- To hear and identify initial sounds in words.
- To use experience of . . . poems . . . as a basis for independent writing . . .

Objectives from the *National Literacy Strategy (Y1)*:

- From YR to practise and secure alphabetic letter knowledge.
- To use rhymes . . . as models for their own writing.

Objectives from the *National Literacy Strategy (Y2)*:

- To reinforce and apply their word-level skills through shared and guided reading.
- To use simple poetry structures and to substitute own ideas, write new lines.

Materials needed

- ■ Enlarged copy of *Funny Jim* (see 'Preparation'), copy of *Wacky Jack* (see 'Preparation'), easel, Blu-tack, flip-chart, marker pens
- ■ Large cartons, covers or sheets, a bike from the outdoor play equipment, trousers, top, gloves and socks, papier mâché mix and balloon to make model's head, paints and paintbrushes, wool or fur fabric, glue, bubble wrap, shoes, paper, pencils or marker pens
- ■ The children's name cards
- ■ 'J' cards (see 'Preparation') and tokens, card, glue, scissors
- ■ Copy of unfinished verse about Funny Jim (see 'Preparation')

Optional materials for other activities

- ■ Card to make a die, with chosen words on each face, scissors, glue
- ■ Card to make word cards, with chosen word on each one

Preparation

- ▲ Enlarge *Wacky Jack*, on Photocopiable Sheet 27 (p. 103) and *Funny Jim* (p. 101) on a photocopier or type them on a computer using 24-point Tahoma, then print them out. Fix *Wacky Jack* to the easel and fix *Funny Jim* on top of it. Put the easel beside the flip-chart.

▲ Use Photocopiable Sheet 28 (p. 104) to make a set of 'J' cards. You could make more cards with other words and/or pictures, according to achievement level. For example, *jar, jungle, jacket, just, job, juice, jet* and so on.

▲ Sort out the children's name cards, paper and pencils or marker pens, flip-chart and marker pens for Group D.

▲ Enlarge Photocopiable Sheet 29 (p. 105) or type it on a computer using 24-point Tahoma, then print it out.

Introducing the poem

- Tell the children you're going to read them a funny poem about some men. Read the title and ask them to guess what might be funny about Jim. Tell them to remember their guess to see later if they were right. Let them just listen to the poem while you read it the first time. Read it to them, using expression and intonation to put across the fun of the words. When you have finished, ask the children whether they thought the poem was funny. Why or why not? Explain that it's fine if they don't find it funny – we don't all laugh at the same things. Which is their favourite verse? Why? Recite the poem again, encouraging the children to join in.

- Explore the text in a little more detail. Can anyone tell you why Jim is funny, why Joe is silly and why John is nosy? Can the children decide who is the strangest person in the poem? Why? What do they notice about the names of the men? Are there any children in the group whose name also begins with J? Can the children tell you something about the pattern of the poem? (The first and second lines are repeated as the fifth and sixth lines of each verse.) Are there any rhyming words? See if the children can say what these are (*Jim/him*; *head/bed*; *Joe/grow*; *hours/flowers*; *John/on*; *do/YOU*).

- Ask the children to help you write another verse for the poem. Uncover the unfinished verse about Jack (*Wacky Jack*) and read it through together, explaining to the children that they're going to fill in the spaces. Because of the pattern and rhythm of the verse they shouldn't find it difficult to suggest rhymes for the existing words. When you have finished the verse, recite it together and then add it to the other verses of *Funny Jim*. Enjoy reciting the whole poem together.

- Can anyone think of other names beginning with J? For example, Josh, Jane, Jacob, Judy, Jethro, Jill, Jerry and Julia. Play around with the poem by substituting the names suggested by the children. Tell them they could change 'man' to 'girl' if they want to use female names. Remind them that this time their poems won't rhyme, but that doesn't matter. Some examples of substituted lines are: *I know a funny man called Jake* and *I know a funny girl called Jane*.

- Be sensitive to children whose names begin with J. Substitute their name only if you're sure they won't mind. Have some fun reciting the new version with the substituted names, remembering to add the extension verse that the children wrote.

Focus activities

Group A: Help the children to make a child-size model of Funny Jim in bed with his bike. Use large cartons and 'sheets' from the Home Corner to make a bed. Stuff the trousers, top, gloves and socks with bubble wrap; make a papier mâché head, using wool or fur fabric for hair; tie the shoes to the head and put the model in the bed with the bike. Let the children write a label, caption and/or sentence(s) about the model.

Group B: Put the tokens and the 'J' cards (face down) on the table and play a game of 'I hear with my little ear', focusing on the letter 'j'. The children take turns to pick a card and look at it before saying *I hear with my little ear a word that begins with 'j'* . . . followed by a clue. For example, if they pick *jumper*, they could say *I hear with my little ear a word that begins with 'j' and it's something warm that you wear in winter*. The child who guesses the word wins a token and whoever has the highest number of tokens at the end wins the game.

Group C: Help the children to write some words that each character in the poem might say. For example, Funny Jim's words could be *I'm funny. I like to wear my shoes on my head and ride my bicycle in bed*. When they have worked out the words, let the children role-play any or all of the characters, speaking their lines. They could record their role-play on a cassette to listen to again later, if they wanted.

Group D: Give the children their name cards and help them to make up some alliterative sentences about themselves. Tell them their sentences can be silly, as long as there are words beginning with their initial letter. For example, Daniel might choose *Daniel danced at dinner time*; Pritpal could say *Pritpal put piles of potatoes in a puddle*; Suzy may write *Silly Suzy stuffed sausages in a smelly sack*. Help them to draft and redraft their sentences on the flip-chart before making their final choice.

Group E: Work with the children to finish the incomplete verse about Funny Jim (Photocopiable Sheet 29). Brainstorm some ideas with them and jot them down on the flip-chart. Experiment with the ideas and then decide on a final version together before filling in the missing words. An example might be:

> I know a funny man called Jim,
> And I am very, very fond of him.
> He wears his trousers on his head
> And eats blue strawberries in bed.
> I know a funny man called Jim,
> And I am very, very fond of him.

Other structured play activities

- Play a variation of 'Simon Says', using *Funny Jim Says* instead. The child who 'survives' the longest is the winner. Use some commands that include 'j' words, such as *Jiggle like a jelly*, *Jump up high* or *Make yourself look like a jug*.
- Make a die and write on each face a chosen letter. Play a game where the children take turns to throw the die and think of a name beginning with the rolled letter. Recite one of the verses from *Funny Jim* using the new name. The verse won't rhyme but that doesn't matter.
- Play 'Funny Jim Lucky Dip'. Put a selection of word cards (your choice), including some beginning with 'j', into Funny Jim's shoe. Pass the shoe around and let the children take out a card. If they can read the word and/or identify the initial phoneme (as required), they keep the card. If they pull out a 'j' card, they can have another dip. The winner is the child with the most cards at the end of the game.

Cousin Peter
Traditional

Last evening Cousin Peter came,
Last evening Cousin Peter came,
Last evening Cousin Peter came
To show that he was here.

He knocked three times upon the door,
He knocked three times upon the door,
He knocked three times upon the door
To show that he was here.

He wiped his feet upon the mat,
He wiped his feet upon the mat,
He wiped his feet upon the mat
To show that he was here.

He hung his hat upon the hook,
He hung his hat upon the hook,
He hung his hat upon the hook
To show that he was here.

He kicked his shoes off one by one,
He kicked his shoes off one by one,
He kicked his shoes off one by one
To show that he was here.

He danced about in stocking feet,
He danced about in stocking feet,
He danced about in stocking feet
To show that he was here.

He made a bow and said goodbye,
He made a bow and said goodbye,
He made a bow and said goodbye
To show that he was gone.

Funny Jim

Barbara Ireson and Christopher Rowe

I know a funny man called Jim,
And I am very, very fond of him.
He wears his shoes upon his head
And rides a bicycle in bed.
I know a funny man called Jim,
And I am very, very fond of him.

I know a silly man called Joe,
Who likes his weeds to grow and grow.
And he will dig for hours and hours
And take up all his lovely flowers.
I know a silly man called Joe,
Who likes his weeds to grow and grow.

I know a nosy man called John,
Who has to know whatever's going on.
What you say, what you do,
Nosy John is watching YOU.
I know a nosy man called John,
Who has to know whatever's going on.

three	feet
mat	hook
shoe	bows
sock	door

Wacky Jack

I know a wacky man called Jack

Who thinks the front is at the ....

He goes upstairs then comes back ....

And when he smiles he wears a ....

I know a wacky man called Jack

Who thinks the front is at the ....

jumper

jelly

jam

jigsaw

jug

jump

I know a funny man called Jim,

And I am very, very fond of him.

He wears his .... on his head

And eats .... in bed.

I know a funny man called Jim,

And I am very, very fond of him.

Observation and assessment for speaking and listening

During the sessions observing the children, you may find it useful to refer to some of these questions as a way of focusing on how their speaking and listening skills are developing.

- Do all children make a contribution to the whole-group or small-group discussion?
- Are the grammatical structures correct? Is the syntax correct?
- Do the children use appropriate vocabulary? Do they use context to work out unfamiliar words?
- Do the children show a curiosity about new words and try to explore how to use them appropriately?
- Is their speech fluent and clear?
- Do the children sustain attention when listening?
- Do they listen with respect to others' views and opinions?
- Do the children take turns in conversations?
- Do they appear to understand what is being said by you and by the other children?
- Do the children ask relevant and appropriate questions about a shared text?
- Do the children have a concept of the sequence of a story?
- Do they use the illustrations for clues about the meaning, sequence and content of the story?
- Do the children talk about key events and characters in a familiar story?
- Are they able to negotiate plans and roles?
- Do they enjoy listening to stories, rhymes and songs, and are they able to respond to them, taking part and using them in their play and learning?
- Do the children use language in their imaginative play? Do they role-play and create imaginary experiences?

Observation and assessment for reading and writing

During your sessions observing the children, you may find it useful to refer to some of these questions as a way of focusing on how their reading and writing skills are developing.

- Can the children hear and say initial and final sounds in words? Can they hear and say short vowel sounds within words?
- Can the children name and sound the letters of the alphabet?
- Do the children know that print in English is read from left to right, and from top to bottom?
- Do the children enjoy exploring and experimenting with sounds, words and texts?
- Do they have a knowledge of the vocabulary of literacy, such as 'book', 'cover', 'page', 'line', 'title', 'author', 'front', 'back', 'word', 'reading', 'writing', etc.?
- Can the children write their own name?
- Do they attempt to write for different purposes, such as letters, lists, instructions, stories, etc.?
- Do the children use their knowledge of phonics to attempt to read or write simple regular words?
- Can they hold and use a pencil appropriately?
- Do they write letters using the correct sequence of movements?
- Can the children recognise the important elements of words such as shape, length and common spelling patterns?
- Do the children use different cues when reading, e.g. their knowledge of a story, context, illustrations, syntax, etc.
- Can they identify significant parts of a text, e.g. captions, characters' names, chants, etc.?
- Are the children aware of the structure of a story, i.e. a beginning, a middle and an end? Are they aware of the actions and consequences within a story?
- Do the children check text for sense? Do they self-correct when something they read does not make sense?
- Can the children identify patterns in stories and poems? Can they extend them?
- Can the children match phonemes to graphemes? Can they write them?
- Do they understand alphabetical order?
- Can the children sight-read familiar words such as captions or high frequency words?